THE BIZFIX

NICHOLAS R. DUVA

ISBN: 1481257676
ISBN 13: 9781481257671

DEDICATION

I'd like to dedicate this book to my wonderful wife, Donna, who has put up with me for over forty years since we first met. She also never complained when I had to be out of town several nights during the week so I could help various companies. She is the reason our two sons, Devin and Justin, grew up to be wonderful husbands and fathers. Donna, I deeply thank you for your love and support. I could not have done any of the things in this book without you. I love you very much.

TABLE OF CONTENTS

ACKNOWLEDGEMENTS

I could not have written this little book without the help of several people. Their insights as to how words could be interpreted and how good books are written were invaluable.

I'd first like to thank my ex-business partner and long time great friend, Michael K. Kelly, for his meticulous review of every word in this book. His straightforward comments were just what I needed.

I'd next like to thank Roger D. McCoy, who has so far worked with me in three different companies, becoming a friend I can call out of the blue and ask if he wants to jump into my current endeavor. He instantly knew which "Real Entrepreneurial Experiences" referred to those companies where we worked together.

I'd also like to thank William K. Hall, the founder of The Executive Committee (now known as Vistage International) on the West Coast. Bill played a role in connecting me with many of the companies with whom I consulted over the past twenty years. He has been a tremendous friend and has the uncanny ability to help me look at a situation from a slightly different perspective that offers illumination to see things more clearly.

Next on the list is Wil Beach, one of the best CEOs I have ever met. I counted on him to find the "chocolate ice cream." He also rightfully reminded me to tell you the reader what I was going to say, say it, and then tell the reader what I said. Wil also was the one who said that after all my friends above gave their very valuable input to go get a professional to make the book become a reality.

I was lucky to meet business author and book writing consultant, Henry DeVries, who made the book much more professional. He became the quarterback who led me through consistency of message and directed me to other professionals who added greatly to the end product.

One of those people to whom Henry directed me was Sharron Stockhausen. She edited the book in accordance with the Chicago Manual of Style; a manual that I didn't even know existed. After Sharron got done I had to reassure myself I really did pay attention in English class. Her business background helped tremendously to refine the message.

Another one of Henry's recommendations was Joni McPherson who designed the front and back covers which I hope you find eye catching. In addition, she made some very hard-to-read figures as clear as possible.

Henry also expedited my trip through Amazon land so folks could actually purchase the book in hard copy or download it to their Kindle.

Finally, I'd like to thank my wife, Donna, who probably has read more books than any person I know. Every time she started a comment with "I know I don't know a lot about business, but ....," I knew I had written something that didn't make a lot of sense.

CHAPTER 1

YOUR TICKET TO FINANCIAL INDEPENDENCE

If you own a business, this is the book your banker, accountant, and attorney want you to read. You can add your spouse and financial planner to the list too.

Most owners of businesses with revenues of $5 million to $50 million have a *dream* of someday achieving financial independence. Financial independence is defined as having enough capital outside of your business to generate the income level you desire for the rest of your life. Your business provides you with two monetary sources for achieving financial independence:

1. The money you take out of the business while you are running it (salary and distributions).
2. The proceeds you receive from selling the business.

Most owners cannot take enough money out of the business while they are running it to achieve their dream. The main reason is that most businesses do not make the significant double digit profits which would be required to do so. Therefore, the owner must build the business to a size where its sale will provide the additional capital.

Your business is simply a means to an end. The end is the achievement of financial independence for life. If you constantly look at your business in this manner, it will keep you focused on the correct issues. This focus will help keep you from taking action for the wrong reasons — for vanity or because the business is your baby. These actions may feel good, but usually don't do anything to improve the value of the business.

Over the last twenty years of my career, I have worked with more than one thousand business owners. I have been the CEO/COO of eleven different companies. These experiences enabled me to learn some of the fundamental principles that apply to all businesses.

People refer to me as a turnaround guy. The reality is that I apply sound business principles to whatever business situation I find. I can apply these principles even when the company is under severe duress. It is kind of like playing offensive and defensive at the same time. Businesses under duress deal with poor cash flow, irate vendors, intolerant bankers, and worried employees. It is much easier to run a business without the duress, but, whether the business is under duress or not, the exact same principles apply. I show you those principles in this book.

While getting to know business owners, whether they became clients or not, I discovered two things:

1. Many business owners *don't know what they don't know* about business, and
2. The owners haven't *practiced* running their business correctly.

In the movie, *Moneyball,* one of the best baseball players who ever played the game, Mickey Mantle, was quoted as saying, "It's unbelievable how much you don't know about the game you've been playing all your life." The same is true about business. There are many reasons this happens. Business schools don't teach the real world of entrepreneurship. Besides, most owners of businesses with revenue of $5 million to $50 million didn't go to business school.

Most owners started with a good idea. Their hard work, intellect, talent, timing, and some luck made the business successful to some degree, but did they really become good at all aspects of running a business? Some of the major areas of business are finance, operations, sales and marketing, purchasing, engineering, customer service, legal, and inventory control. Most entrepreneurs never really become good at all of those items.

Brains and talent will only take you so far. Many people think if they have some talent and continuously work hard, they will succeed. In his book *Outliers* (Gladwell 2008), Malcolm Gladwell points out that the closer psychologists look at the careers of the gifted, the smaller the role innate talent seems to play and the bigger role preparation seems to play. Gladwell notes:

The idea that excellence at performing a complex task requires a critical minimum level of practice surfaces again and again in studies of expertise. In fact, researchers have settled on what they believe is the magic number for true expertise: ten thousand hours.

What separates elite violinists from "good" violinists who only end up music teachers? Practice. 10,000 hours to be exact. Why is Bill Gates able to take baths in hundred dollar bills? He spent hours upon hours (hello, 10,000) honing his computer programming skills as a high school student.

Do business owners practice the correct things? It is a slightly facetious question. If you don't know all the things you need to do to make a business successful, how can you practice them? If you haven't run a business three times as large as your current business, how do you practice those things it takes to grow your business to that level? Most business owners do what they think is correct. They are confident in their own decisions because most business owners are confident in themselves. If they weren't, they probably wouldn't own the business. Unfortunately, if they are only slightly wrong (not necessarily catastrophically), they will be doing the same things repeatedly that won't take them to where they want to go.

No one can go it alone. Gladwell points out in *Outliers* that "to be successful you need a community around you that prepares you for the world. No one – not rock stars, not professional athletes, not software billionaires, and not even geniuses – ever makes it alone." It is not only smart to get help in running your business; it will greatly increase the chances of achieving your dream.

For most entrepreneurs who know what they are doing, their business will be the main source of the capital to achieve their dream of financial independence. Chapter 9 - The End Game shows how to do the calculations to figure what is needed to achieve that dream and how to calculate what the value of the business needs to be.

Using the techniques in this book will enable you to increase the value of your business while providing downside protection against things you can't control, like the economy.

In each chapter I have included some "Real Entrepreneurial Experiences." These experiences happened in real businesses. The point of each of these experiences is to show the following:

1. The situation that existed.
2. How it was negatively impacting the business.
3. The action taken to change the situation.
4. The result of the changes.

Business owners need to excel in three key areas that are critical – cash flow, operational efficiency, and the business model. In each of these areas the owners must apply ferocious discipline, focus on what is important in each area, and create processes that assure the right things are repeatedly done correctly.

If you concentrate on the three key areas in your business, you will greatly increase the chances of achieving your dream.

CHAPTER 1 HIGHLIGHTS

1. Your business can be the ticket to your financial independence dream.
2. Many business owners don't know what they don't know.
3. Most business owners have not practiced running their business correctly.
4. No one can go it alone. Getting the correct advice increases the chances of achieving your dream.

CHAPTER 2

THE TURNAROUND MYTH

Too many business owners think a turnaround is when a large public company that has been poorly managed hires a specialist to whom they pay millions of dollars to fire thousands of workers. This perception is too extreme and too limited. If we use the following two definitions, we put "turnaround" in the proper perspective:

1. Turnaround (noun) – a movement in a new direction
2. Turnaround (verb) – improve significantly

If business owners look at a turnaround using these two definitions, they should realize their business should continuously be going through a turnaround. My experience shows the following approximate breakdown of businesses with sales in the range of $5 million to $50 million:

1. Less than 10 percent of the businesses will perform so the owners achieve their dream of personal financial independence.
2. More than 30 percent of these businesses will die, either quickly or excruciatingly slowly, where the owner loses more than just the business.
3. The remaining 60 percent remain alive, but the owners will not achieve their dream of personal financial independence.

French Foreign Legion

To be able to accomplish a successful turnaround, your company needs the discipline of the French Foreign Legion. According to *March or Die – the Heroic Foreign Legion* (Lookandlearn 2012), the French Foreign Legion was almost totally destroyed during a civil war in Spain in the 1830s. When the Legion tried to reform, only sixty-three men signed on.

The image and tradition of the Legion was changed through ferocious discipline, primarily through marching. The Legion's daily routine consisted of marching up to thirty miles in the Saharan sun carrying a one-hundred-pound load so each was self sufficient. For five hours, they would march, counter march, musket drill, and mock battle. This routine led to the Legion's slogan of "March or Die" and made the French Foreign Legion into one of the toughest fighting forces in the world. This is a great example of a turnaround story.

Turnaround or Die

Using the definitions of "turnaround" in the opening of this chapter, if business owners are not constantly turning around their businesses their dream will die. If owners want to achieve their dream, they must be exceptional performers in the following three areas:

1. **Cash Flow** – This is the most important fundamental to know in business. It is highly likely business owners will not be able to grow their business to achieve their dream, if they do not understand cash flow.
2. **Operational Efficiency** – Operational efficiency is absolutely necessary for on-time delivery, to keep costs low, and to provide customers with what they want. The business will not be able to grow to the needed value to fulfill the dream without operational efficiency.
3. **Business Model** – Business owners *must* continuously examine their business model to see if it still makes sense. One of the biggest mistakes business owners make is to keep doing what they have always done even when it doesn't work anymore.

Failure to execute in any one of these three areas is the biggest mistake that can kill your business. Failure to execute in all three areas guarantees business failure.

Since so few owners achieve their dream, some discussion about the "die" part is appropriate here. There are two ways to die – a simple failure or a crash and burn. If you recognize a business will not work, you must shut it down and preserve your other personal assets. You have simply failed, but you will live to do something else to capture your dream.

The other way for a business to die is when owners decide to keep pouring good money after bad and put everything they have accumulated outside the business back into it. In addition, they borrow more money from other sources and then lose all of that as well. This is a crash-and-burn scenario from which the owner will never recover and the dream dies.

Now let's concentrate on the success part —the Turnaround. There is no such thing as coasting when trying to improve or grow a business. In each of the major areas of cash flow, operational efficiencies, and the business model, the following must be done:

1. Business owners must have a *ferocious discipline.* My definition of ferocious discipline is repeatedly doing the things you need to do to be successful, even if you don't like to do them. In other words, you are so disciplined that the correct, most important things *always* get done.
2. Develop the *processes* that allow your employees to produce your product or service with consistent quality.
3. Be able to *focus* on the things that deliver the profitable goods and/or services your clients want to buy from you.

Ferocious Discipline

You are the owner of a business. No one tells you when to get to work. No one tells you how long to stay at work. No one tells you what to work on when you are at work. This is really cool. It is also why business owners need ferocious discipline.

Unfortunately, it probably should be called ferocious self-discipline. How many people do you know that you can say that person has a lot of self-discipline? Not many, I expect. This is one of the reasons for chapter 12 – Get Help with Your Fix. We are all humans. Self-discipline is hard. That is why some of us don't exercise, some don't eat a balanced diet, and some don't lead balanced lives.

It would be great if you, and every reader of this book, would become the Navy Seals of business, but that won't happen. If you want to achieve your dream, you will develop ferocious discipline through the right combination of self-discipline and allow proven advisors to hold you accountable for maintaining discipline.

It is actually pretty easy in business to identify all the things that should be done. The real trick to good management is to select and prioritize the most important items.

I've already said the most important items are those that improve cash flow, operational efficiency, and maintaining the proper business model. Everything else is secondary.

This is not saying that you skip the other things that have to be accomplished by a certain time. It is stating that the three major areas come first and everything is done at the end of the day, at night, or on the weekend. Welcome to the world of the business owner who is using the business as a means to an end of establishing financial independence dream.

Processes

Establishing processes is what will lead you to operational efficiency. Here is an example that is familiar to most of us. How many ways does McDonald's make their French fries? *One. Only one.* You can go into any McDonald's and the fries taste the same. It really doesn't matter whether you personally like them or not (I like them too much). McDonald's has decided that if they make fries a particular way, their customers will pay the price for which McDonald's wants to sell them. McDonald's demands that its franchisee maintain ferocious discipline to make sure the fries taste exactly the same way in all McDonald's. Therefore, McDonald's created a foolproof process to deliver French fries to their customers.

Let's see how McDonald's makes it easy to maintain the discipline. Here is a list of what their store owners do *not* have to do:

1. They don't have to pick the potatoes.
2. They don't have to cut the potatoes.
3. They don't have to wash the potatoes.
4. They don't have to season the potatoes.
5. They don't have to get rid of the potato skins.
6. They don't have to time the cooking cycle.

What do the McDonald's employees have to do?

1. Open the bag of potatoes.
2. Pour the contents into the frying basket.
3. Push the button.

What is the one thing the employees have discretion to do and when they don't do it correctly customers get irritated? When the buzzer goes off signifying the potatoes are done, please go turn off that darn buzzer and take out the fries.

If you maintain ferocious discipline to perform a process as instructed, customers get what they want to buy every time. In the "Real Entrepreneurial Experiences" below are examples of processes that were changed in five different businesses in five different industries. Some of these changes were just common sense, but it took someone from outside the business to be able to see what common sense to apply.

REAL ENTREPRENEURIAL EXPERIENCE

Situation: Orders for next day delivery were taken until 4:00 p.m.

Issue: Production could not make all the products by 6:00 a.m. next morning when delivery trucks were supposed to leave the dock. Order fulfillment was only 77 percent.

Resolution: Cutoff time for next day orders was changed to 1:00 p.m.

Result: Order fulfillment rate went to 99 percent.

Situation: Sales people chased small medical studies ($5,000) in hopes of larger follow-on studies.

Issue: All small studies lost a significant amount of money. No follow-on studies were occurring.

Resolution: Minimum study size was raised to $50,000.

Result: All studies turned profitable. Company sold for twice the amount that was expected.

Situation: Cash collected from coin operated machines deposited over thirty days after collections.

Issue: Corporate cash flow very poor. There were significant theft losses.

Resolution: Cash collected from coin operated machines had to be deposited within twenty-four hours.

Result: Theft was significantly reduced. Cash flow to corporate greatly improved.

Situation: Manufacturing process started regardless if all needed material was available.

Issue: Product taken offline then put online, then again taken offline when material wasn't available for next

THE TURNAROUND MYTH   11

stage. Production labor costs were very high. Product quality was very low. Warranty costs were very high.
Resolution: Do not start manufacturing until all materials are in house. Adjust delivery expectations accordingly.
Result: Greatly reduced labor costs. Product quality improved tremendously, vastly reducing warranty costs.

5. **Situation:** Manufacturing finalized for delivery whichever product was ready first.
Issue: Too many products were ready early. Too many products were late. Few products were delivered on time.
Resolution: Establish dock dates for products to insure on-time or early delivery.
Result: Products manufactured according to need, not speed. On-time delivery rate was greatly improved. Reduced production labor costs. Reduced delivery costs.

What do all of the above "Real Entrepreneurial Experiences" have in common? A *process* was established that, when religiously followed, resulted in consistent, reproducible success.

Focus

Developing a *ferocious discipline* to *focus* on cash flow and their business model seems to be very hard for many business owners. Unfortunately, cash flow and the business model are the two areas that require the most focus. Most business owners look at cash flow as an accounting issue that their bookkeeper will do. This is a terrible mistake.

Focus on the business model requires the examination of something the owner already decided upon. Most business owners seem to have a hard time admitting they were correct at one point, but now the course they chose isn't working.

Focus is something that is easily lost because the business owner is too busy working on things that are necessary, but not important. Michael Gerber's lesson in his book, *The E Myth* (Gerber 1995), said it best many years ago: "Work on your business, not in it." Oftentimes the owner is the only person who can do certain tasks. This fact does not relieve the owner from spending the necessary time to focus on those issues that truly are the ones that really make money for the business.

So how do you know what things require your *focus*? Let's look at something that becomes the basis for examining the business model. Business owners must understand why customers buy from them. Few businesses have the luxury of selling a proprietary product that no one else sells. If that is the case in your business, congratulations and skip to the next chapter. If not, join the crowd of most businesses. If you think the answer regarding why customers buy from you is because you are the cheapest, watch out because your prices will keep going down. It is better if your reasons for customers buying from your company come from the following list:

1. You deliver a good quality product at a fair price in a time frame satisfactory to the customer.
2. You make it easy for your customer to buy your product.
3. You always stand behind your product. If there is a problem, you correct it quickly.
4. The people of your organization who interface with customers treat those customers with respect and make the customers feel important.

Now you must translate these items into specific tasks. For all of these items, you must focus on this simple phrase:

Inspect what you expect.

Let's look at the quality of what you deliver to customers whether it is a product or a service. Do you actually have quality inspectors? If not, then you have to take time to actually look at what your business is sending out. It would be nice if you had dedicated employees who always took pride in what they did. Employee pride does not happen by itself. You have to develop a culture that promotes pride in what is being done.

Start with cleanliness. If you personally don't show that you are a fanatic about having a clean environment, the employees will not believe you care about the product. Start with the employees' restroom. If it is dirty, it sends the message that you don't care about the employees.

Next, time should always be allotted before the end of every shift to clean the production floor. About five to fifteen minutes before the end of the shift, the business owner (you) should go walk the line and see if it is clean. Whenever you walk on the floor during the day, bend over and pick up a piece of paper, wood, or a bolt. Don't walk past it.

Your employees start to notice that cleanliness is important to you, so it will become important to them. Now you have set a good foundation for discussions about pride in the product quality. You must create an environment where the quality of the product is important to the employees. They must believe the product or service provided by your company reflects on them. You need to get the employees to the point that they will not let something leave the facility that is below their standards. Their standard should become high enough that no customers could possibly be dissatisfied. You must constantly *inspect* that the quality is consistent with *what you expect*. If you decided quality is an important issue to your customers, then you establish a *ferocious discipline* to constantly *focus* on making sure it is happening.

Below is a "Real Entrepreneurial Experience" where ferocious discipline about cleanliness led to more than $1 million reduction in warranty work.

REAL ENTREPRENEURIAL EXPERIENCE

Situation: Workers did not understand nor care about the quality of the products.

Issue: Warranty work cost more than $1 million per year.

Resolution: Started by giving strict instructions about how the employees' restroom should be spotlessly cleaned every day. Every day owner personally inspected the restrooms. Employees took notice that management was serious about cleanliness. After the restroom stayed clean every day, discussions about product quality were started. Quality was drilled down to every supervisor. The engineers were sent out to the production line to inspect the various stages to make sure they were in compliance with their drawings. Sales people had to inspect the finished product before it was shipped.

Result: Warranty worked dropped from $1 million to $100,000.

Another area on which to *focus* is on-time delivery. You must look to see (inspect) if you are delivering when you said you would. Here's an example of how quickly we were able to turnaround a situation to the customer's delight:

REAL ENTREPRENEURIAL EXPERIENCE

Situation: Product delivery dates to customers were consistently late. Major customer started sending orders to competitors.

Issue: There was no process or paperwork to give visibility to the production manager as to when certain products needed to be on the dock to enable them to be delivered on time to the customer.

Resolution: Production paperwork issued to ensure products were ready when they were promised to the customer, not whichever product could be made most quickly.

Result: Picture below tells the tale. Customer increased orders to higher level than before. Notice how quickly late deliveries virtually disappeared and the early deliveries started to soar.

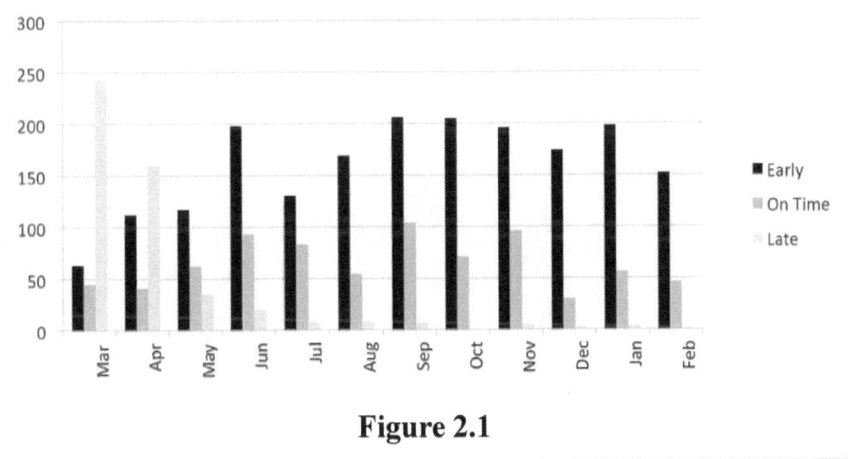

Figure 2.1

In summary, business owners must apply ferocious discipline, develop processes; and focus on three major areas – cash flow, operational efficiencies, and the business model.

CHAPTER 2 HIGHLIGHTS

1. If a business owner is not constantly in a turnaround mode, the dream for financial independence will die.
2. The business owner must be an exceptional performer in three major areas— cash flow, operational efficiency, and updating the business model.
3. In each of the major areas, the business owner must have ferocious discipline; develop processes to achieve operational efficiencies; and maintain intensive focus on what is important.

CHAPTER 3

DATA, REPORTS, AND MEANING

Before business owners can develop ferocious discipline, they must make sure of the following:

1. The data upon which they depending are correct and reliable.
2. The data mean what they think it means.

In many cases, the data that management are using fall into one of the following categories:

1. The data are insufficient to draw the conclusions they are reaching.
2. The data are irrelevant.
3. The data are not timely.
4. The data mix apples and oranges, so all conclusions are meaningless.
5. The data are simply a compilation of facts from which no one could draw a conclusion.
6. The data are incorrect.

There are several reasons the above situations happen. Throughout this chapter the "Real Entrepreneurial Experiences" will reference the items above. In some cases the method used for measuring something was correct in the beginning of the company, but today the data are incorrect for what you are trying to monitor.

I'll explain with a "Real Entrepreneurial Experience".

REAL ENTREPRENEURIAL EXPERIENCE

Situation (Items 1, 6): Company tracked how many square feet of product was produced daily to control labor costs.

Issue: When the company started, they only made their product out of one kind of material. If they produced "x" square feet of the product and sold it for "y" dollars per square foot, they would have "x" times "y" in sales. The company should make the target gross profit if the labor costs were below 19 percent of the sales dollars. They then started producing the product out of three different types of material. The number of square feet produced every day no longer had a direct correlation to sales because the pricing was completely different for each type of material.

Resolution: Company started tracking sales dollars of product produced, not square footage.

Result: Production manager now held responsible to perform to a meaningful metric: sales dollars versus labor costs expended.

Financial statements are a prime example of data that are not timely (Item 3.) Ideally, you get your financial statements within ten days of the end of the month.

Unfortunately, many owners are lucky to get the statements before the end of the following month. To add to the problem, the data being reviewed is thirty to sixty days old and nothing can be done about it.

The subject of mixing apples and oranges requires some thinking to reveal the discrepancy (Item 4.) The golden rule is to align costs and revenues in the same reporting period. Service organizations frequently misalign their expenses and revenue when projects take multiple months to complete and no revenue is declared until the project is over. Some owners say this misalignment tends to even out over time when in reality *it never corrects itself.* Owners of construction companies and some manufacturers try to align revenues and costs by reporting revenues on a percentage-of-completion method. This is a method to claim revenue that you have not billed, but for which costs have been incurred.

> **Red Alert: Derek Sivers once said, "Fish don't know they are in water." The industry you are in and your business culture create biases. Experienced consultants do not look at your business the same way you do. This allows them to see things from a different perspective often giving you more clarity about what the data really say.**

Below are several real entrepreneurial examples that give owners data they should not use to make decisions.

REAL ENTREPRENEURIAL EXPERIENCE

Situation (Items 1, 4): The sales are recorded for each work day of the month (say twenty-three days), but wages are recorded for only the pay periods of the month (say two, representing twenty days).
Issue: This usually indicates two profitable months followed by an unprofitable one. The Profit & Loss Statements for all three months are incorrect.
Resolution: Wages accrued so they match the actual working days of the month.
Result: Financial statements reformatted to match revenues and expenses relative to labor.

2. **Situation (Items 1, 3, 4, 6):** Service firm works on projects over multiple months, expensing employee wages every month, but only recording income revenue at the end of the project when they are paid.
    Issue: Revenue does not match expenses in the same time period.
    Resolution: Company changed to recognizing revenue on a percentage completion basis.
    Result: Financial statements now match revenues and expenses relative to labor.

3. **Situation (Items 2, 3, 4, 5):** Items are purchased in month one to support sales in that month, but the vendor invoice doesn't come in until month two so those purchases are recorded in the wrong month.
    Issue: Revenue does not match expenses in the same time period.
    Resolution: Bookkeeping either accrues the expenses or requests invoice from vendor in time to provide financials in accurate time.
    Result: Financial statements now match revenues and expenses relative to labor.

4. **Situation (Items 1, 5, 6):** Cash flow projections should be done for six months in the future.
    Issue: Cash flow was not predictable two weeks into the future, so six-month projections were a total waste of time.
    Resolution: Bookkeeping tracked cash flow daily with projections for only two weeks in advance.
    Result: Company knew exactly what it could pay and when.

5. **Situation (Items 1, 6):** Short-term "blips" in revenue are explained as seasonal or blamed on unexpected temperatures.
Issue: Revenue shortfall was not due to seasonality; it was actually a continuation of a long-term trend.
Resolution: The tracking of revenue was changed to fifty-two-week trailing.
Result: Owner made much better pricing decisions to reverse revenue slide.

6. **Situation (Items 1, 5, 6):** Company used the term "offline" to mean the product was complete or simply taken offline because material was missing.
Issue: No one could tell why a product was offline or how close it was to being completed. Keeping the customer informed about delivery dates was almost impossible.
Resolution: No product was allowed to be put online if material was missing. When a product was taken offline, it meant it was in final preparation for delivery.
Result: Product quality improved. On-time delivery rates improved.

7. **Situation (Items 1, 2, 5):** Small company paid taxes on the cash basis, so tried to manage company using cash basis financial statements.
Issue: Management could not tell what was happening financially based on cash basis financial statements.
Resolution: Part time bookkeeper hired to create accrual accounting financial statements.
Results: Management was much more effective once they could see what was really happening.

8. **Situation (Items 1, 2, 5):** Company with eight different stores did not separate costs of goods sold and gross profit by store.
    Issue: Company could not tell if one or all of the stores were underperforming.
    Resolution: Costs of goods sold tracked by stores.
    Result: Discovered two stores significantly underperforming due to poor pricing and inventory losses. Changes instituted that greatly improved overall performance.

What data should business owners review to increase the chances of achieving their dream? There are three categories: financial data, operational data that shows whether what should be done is being done as it should be done, and bank data. The form in which the data are presented is also important. Most people cannot just look at numbers and draw the appropriate conclusions. Graphs can be extremely important in helping to recognize what is really happening in a business. Chapter 6 discusses the details of how to look at financial statements.

This chapter shows what should be graphed. Let's look at your monthly data:

Financial Data - Monthly

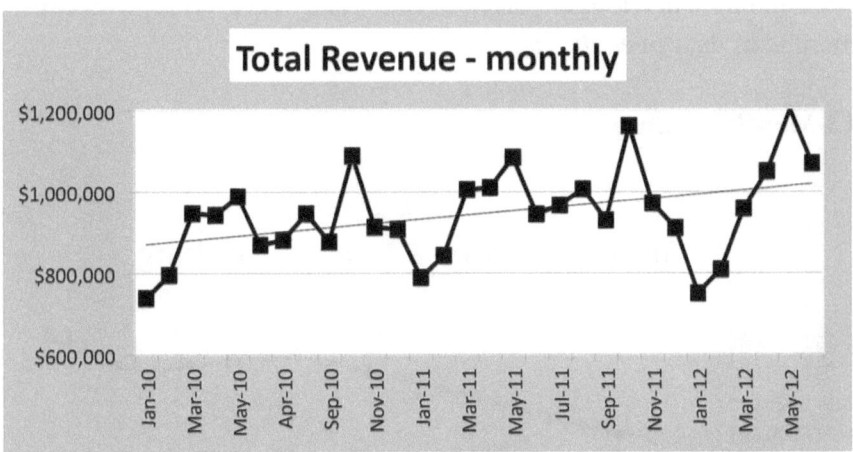

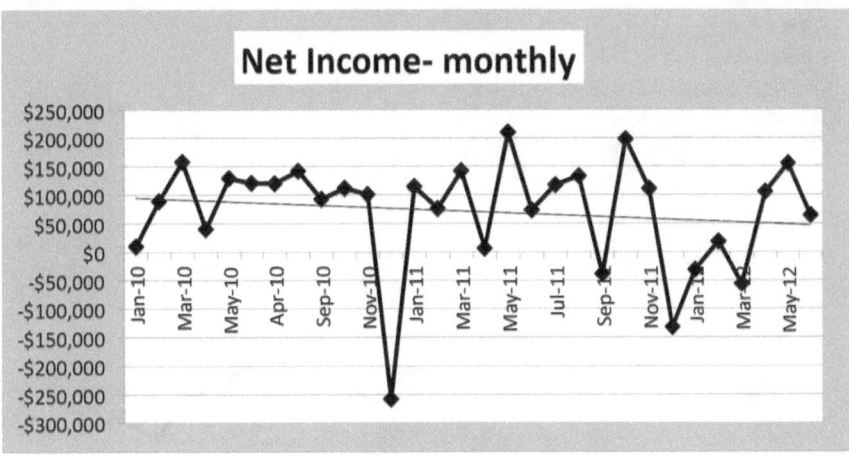

Figure 3.1

These graphs are shocking in their own right, but also generate a lot of questions. The revenue seems to be on an upward trend while profits are in a downward trend. Why is revenue bouncing all over the place? Why does the net income (profit) in December take such a dive while December revenue is not that bad? It is imperative to step back and look at a longer period of time. The next graph shows twelve months of data *in each data point*.

12-Month Trailing

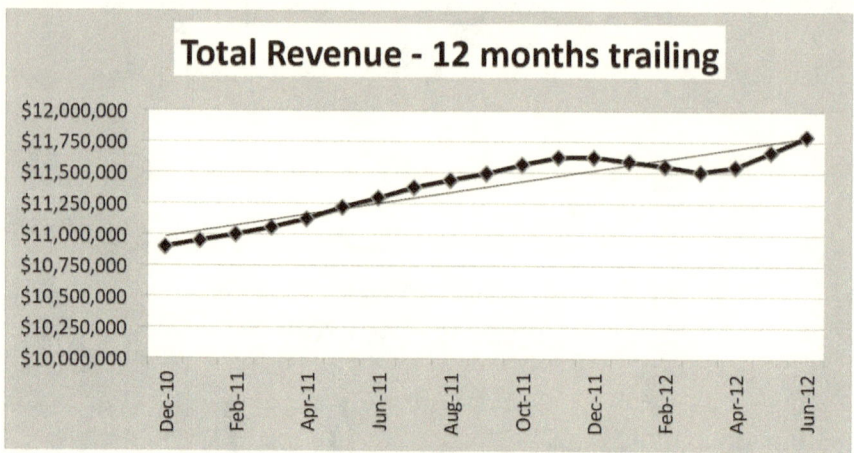

Figure 3.2

It takes some practice to understand the differences between the monthly graphs and the twelve-month trailing graphs. The monthly graphs have thirty months on the X axis while the X axis on the twelve-month trailing graphs contains nineteen months. In fact, both sets of graphs cover the same time period, January 1, 2010 through June 30, 2012. Figure 3.3 shows that each data point on the monthly graphs contains one month of data. On the twelve-month trailing graphs, the Dec-10 represents the period from January 1, 2010 to December 31, 2010. The revenue number for Dec-10 on the twelve-month trailing graph is $10,899,844 versus $908,255 for Dec-10 on the monthly graph (a year of revenue versus a month.)

Data points on 12-month trailing graph		Data points on monthly graph					
		Jan-10	$738,823				
		Feb-10	$795,726	Feb-10	$795,726		
		Mar-10	$947,326	Mar-10	$947,326	Mar-10	$947,326
		Apr-10	$943,091	Apr-10	$943,091	Apr-10	$943,091
		May-10	$988,996	May-10	$988,996	May-10	$988,996
		Jun-10	$869,725	Jun-10	$869,725	Jun-10	$869,725
		Jul-10	$881,909	Jul-10	$881,909	Jul-10	$881,909
		Aug-10	$946,523	Aug-10	$946,523	Aug-10	$946,523
		Sep-10	$877,150	Sep-10	$877,150	Sep-10	$877,150
		Oct-10	$1,089,128	Oct-10	$1,089,128	Oct-10	$1,089,128
		Nov-10	$913,192	Nov-10	$913,192	Nov-10	$913,192
		Dec-10	$908,255	Dec-10	$908,255	Dec-10	$908,255
Dec -10 (1/1/10 thru 12/31/10)	$10,899,844		$10,899,844	Jan-11	$789,163	Jan-11	$789,163
Jan -11 (2/1/10 thru 1/31/11)	$10,950,184				$10,950,184	Feb-11	$842,863
Feb -11 (3/1/10 thru 2/28/11)	$10,997,321						$10,997,321

Figure 3.3

The twelve-month trailing graphs tell us this company has had problems for a long time and nothing was done to stop the slide. Most likely the business owner never saw the data in this form. Some owners like to talk about the monthly (figure 3.1) ups and downs are being caused by seasonality. The twelve-month trailing graphs have all seasons in them, thereby eliminating seasonality as a reason for things happening.

There is an additional set of graphs that should always be reviewed: the three-month trailing graphs.

3-Month Trailing

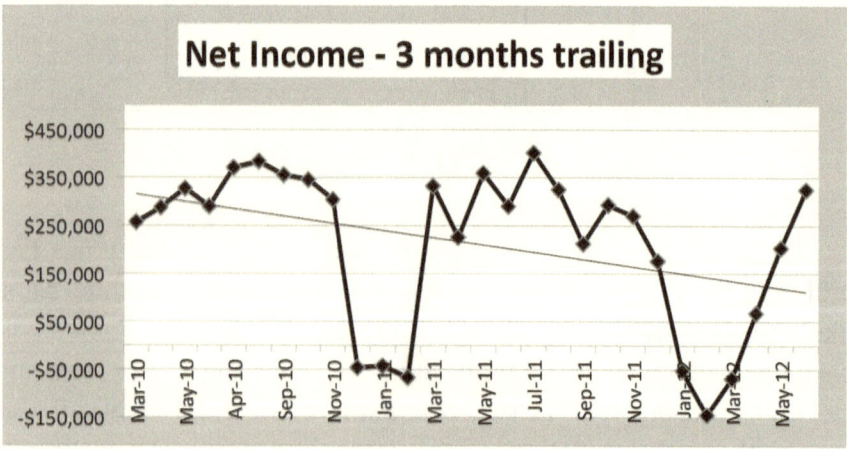

Figure 3.4

These graphs show the short-term revenue is relatively flat and the net income trend is poor. The same data is used in all three sets of graphs, January 1, 2010 through June 30, 2012, just grouped differently. The same kind of explanation made for the twelve-month graphs is necessary for the three-month graphs. May-10 on the three-month graphs represents the period from January 1, 2010 through March 31, 2010. Figure 3.5 shows the translation from monthly data to three-month data.

Data points on 3-month trailing graph		Data points on monthly graph						
		Jan-10	$738,823					
		Feb-10	$795,726	Feb-10	$795,726			
		Mar-10	$947,326	Mar-10	$947,326	Mar-10	$947,326	
Mar -10 (1/1/10 thru 3/31/10)	$2,481,875		$2,481,875	Apr-10	$943,091	Apr-10	$943,091	
Apr -10 (2/1/10 thru 4/30/10)	$2,686,143				$2,686,143	May-10	$988,996	
May -10 (3/1/10 thru 5/31/10)	$2,879,413						$2,879,413	

Figure 3.5

Business owners should be reviewing graphs for the following periods:

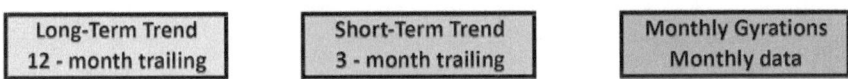

Figure 3.6

The graphs are shown below:

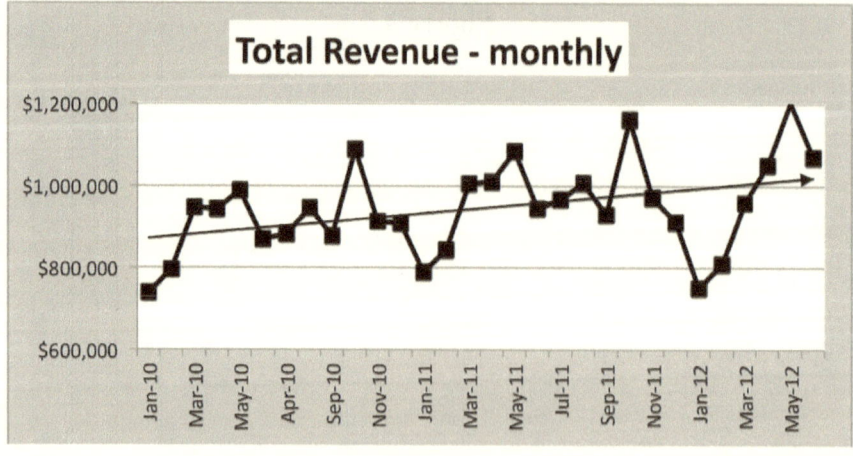

Figure 3.7

Below you can see monthly, three-month trailing, and twelve-month trailing all together, but we are not done.

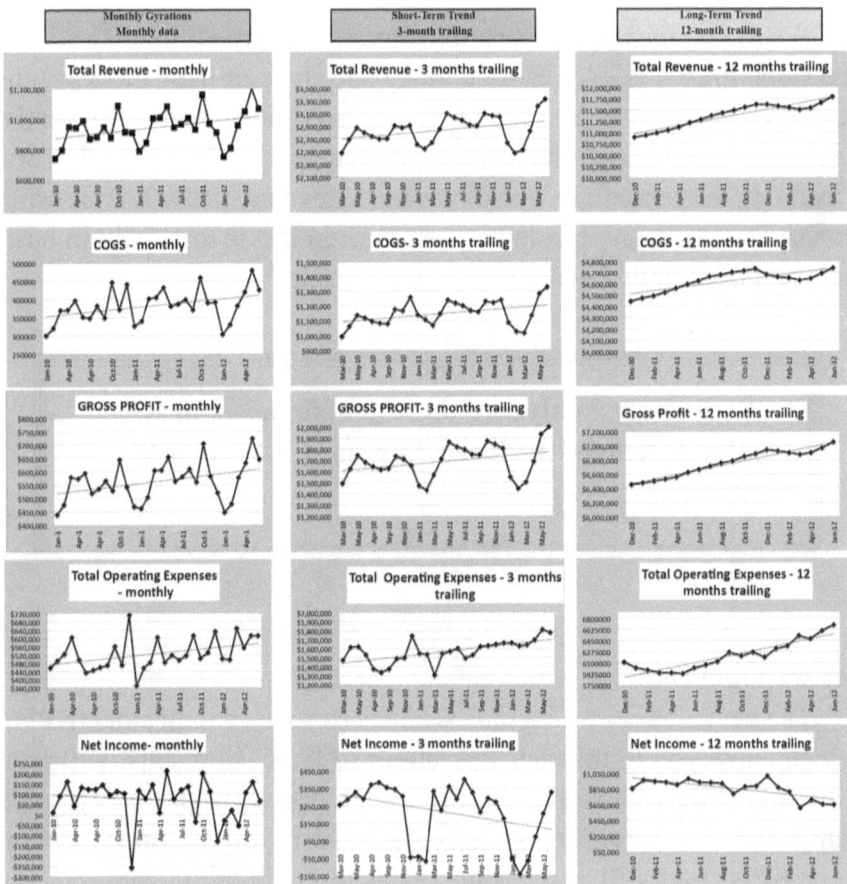

Figure 3.8

Three additional graphs have been added to each of the areas: Cost of Goods Sold (COGS), Gross Profit (Total Revenue minus COGS), and Total Operating Expenses. The details of these areas will be addressed in later chapters.

When you look at this data together, it is pretty telling. By adding the slope lines it is even more telling. The slope of the COGS graphs seem to be parallel to the revenue graphs, so COGS are going up at the same rate as revenue. The biggest problem for this company is Total Operating Expenses are out of control. Revenue growth is slowing down. This company has to be reengineered if it is to remain in business and eventually become attractive for sale.

> **Red Alert: Analyzing these graphs takes practice. You need to learn how they *should* look and why.**

Operational Data

The next area regarding data is key performance indicators (KPIs), which allow you to translate operations to financial results. KPIs can be vastly different from company to company. The trick is to pick things that will more or less guarantee that if you are on track with your KPIs; you will make your financial goals. KPIs can get very "micro" and in many cases are measured daily or at least weekly.

Below are a couple of examples:

Date	Freq	Item	Goal	Current	Last	2 Ago	3 Ago
					Period		
Nov	Weekly	Direct Labor	< 14.5%	14.4%	14.5%	14.6%	14.8%
Nov	Weekly	Payroll/Revenue	< 25.0%	24.4%	25.2%	25.8%	27.0%
Nov	Monthly	YTD Warranty	< 1.0%	0.67%	0.75%	0.74%	0.80%

Figure 3.9

In this case the items are tracked on different frequencies. For this company, management of labor, both direct and total, were extremely important for success. If the warranty came in less than 1 percent, it was apparent that the quality of the product was holding up.

In Figure 3.10, the KPIs are tracked every day to ensure the manufacturing stages are moving like a super highway.

Date	$ Into Assbl	Top Coat Total $$$	Total $ Hinging
4/2	$62,729	$62,301	$43,947
4/3	$36,874	$37,691	$50,701
4/4	$38,047	$48,847	$44,038
4/5	$47,094	$46,223	$51,334
4/6	$49,253	$49,700	$49,866
4/9	$53,885	$56,885	$44,320
4/10	$32,636	$54,341	$44,430
4/11	$26,547	$33,839	$37,127
4/12	$46,526	$36,572	$41,902
4/13	$42,849	$51,782	$47,449
4/16	$23,824	$44,705	$32,184
4/17	$60,961	$43,966	$44,572
4/18	$50,481	$47,488	$44,702
4/19	$48,206	$39,182	$42,462
4/20	$42,793	$36,827	$36,132
4/23	$54,719	$36,208	$30,721
4/24	$7,176	$62,938	$40,627
4/25	$49,921	$49,229	$51,379
4/26	$54,561	$49,910	$54,182

Figure 3.10

> **Red Alert: Make sure you understand that you should pick a KPI to give you a signal when something is out of line. When you see the signal, you must be able to make changes immediately to get back on track to achieve your goals.**

Bank Data

An additional category of data that every owner must review is bank data. Bank data basically show if the company is in compliance with loan covenants. It is best if these data are reviewed no less frequently than quarterly, but it is easy for your accounting people to give data to you monthly with your financial statements. Here is an example:

BANK COVENANTS		
	Covenant	**Current**
Tangible Effective Net Worth	> $4.25M	$4.69M
Leverage Ratio (Debt to Equity)	< 3.0	2.5
Cash Flow Coverage	> 1.25	11.99
Quick Ratio	> 0.5	1.1

Figure 3.10

The problem with the bank covenants is they are not things that owners easily connect directly to the operation of the business. These covenants are usually in place so the bank feels comfortable that their loan is in good hands. You don't usually sit around the office and think about how your tangible net worth is doing. You should know how these covenants are calculated, their meaning, and why they are important to the bank.

Tangible Effective Net Worth = Total Assets minus Goodwill
minus Intangible Assets minus Total Liabilities

The tangible effective net worth covenant shows the bank that
there is sufficient value that the bank could liquidate the company's
assets to pay back the loan. It also ensures the bank that the owner is
not taking too much cash out of the business. Intangible assets are not
physical even though they have value. Goodwill is usually associated
with value of an acquisition due to its reputation, which adds to its
sale price.

Leverage Ratio = Total Liabilities divided by Shareholder's Equity

The leverage ratio tells the bank how burdened the company is
with debt. It also tells them that the owner has skin in the game and
not just the bank.

Cash Flow Coverage = Earnings before interest, taxes,
depreciation, and amortization (EBITDA) divided by principal
payments, interest payments, plus lease payments

The cash flow coverage basically tells the bank the business has
plenty of cash flow to make payments given everything else borrowed
or leased.

Quick Ratio = Cash plus Short-term Investments plus Accounts
Receivable divided by Current Liabilities

The Quick Ratio is simply a very conservative measure of liquid-
ity. This ratio shows the bank the company's ability to handle short-
term issues without disrupting payments to them.

Business owners must look at all three categories of data: financial
data; operational data; and bank data. Owners must know the data
are really telling them what they think it does. They must also figure
out they are looking at the important things. It takes practice and the
ability to disconnect yourself from what always worked before when
circumstances dictate you must do so.

> **Red Alert: The connection between bank cove-nants and operations is not always intuitive.**

CHAPTER 3 HIGHLIGHTS

1. Make sure you are reviewing three types of data: financial, operational, and bank data.
2. In the financial area use monthly, three-month trailing, and twelve-month trailing data in graphical form.
3. Establish Key Performance Indicators to which you can quickly react, making changes to enable you to obtain your goals.
4. Understand the relationship between bank covenants and operational actions.

CHAPTER 4

CASH FLOW

Now that we have set the standard for receiving and looking at the correct data, we must apply that concept to the three major areas: cash flow, operational efficiency, and business model. We will start with cash flow because it is the most important aspect to master in business. I don't care what you have read, or what you have heard, or what you believe – cash flow is the most important aspect to master in business. It will allow you to optimize operations; it will save you during bad times; and it will ultimately determine the value of your business.

Unfortunately, too many business owners believe that if their profit and loss statement (P & L) shows a profit, then their cash flow is fine. No one can determine cash flow from a P & L. There is a pretty simple reason why. The major operational cash flow drivers are the changes in:

1. Accounts Receivable
2. Accounts Payable
3. Inventory
4. Fixed Assets

You find these items on your balance sheet, not your P & L. Most business owners look at their P&L far more than they look at their balance sheet. To make matters worse, owners need to look at two balance sheets because one balance sheet is not enough. At least two balance sheets must be used because

The changes in your balance sheet from the beginning of a period to the end of a period equal the cash flow for that period.

Therefore, at least two balance sheets must be used to compare the changes.

Most accounting software packages will provide a cash flow statement, which is fine to use once you understand where the numbers are really coming from and what they mean. Figure 4.1 shows the output of an accounting system.

Traditional Accounting Program Output

Traditional Accounting Program Output

CASH FLOW	Month 2
OPERATING ACTIVITIES	
Net Income	50,336
Adjustments to reconcile Net Income	
to net cash provided by operations:	
10510 - A/R, Customers	(58,092)
10520 - A/R, Affiliate	1,156
12001 - Raw Materials Inventory	4,800
12002 - Work in Process Inventory	(3,294)
12003 - Finished Goods Inventory	(11,284)
12004 - Supplies Inventory	(2,336)
20001 - Accounts Payable, Vendors	39,024
20007 - A/P Other	18,657
Net cash provided by Operating Activities	38,967
INVESTING ACTIVITIES	
Net cash provided by Investing Activities	24,788
FINANCING ACTIVITIES	
Net cash provided by Financing Activities	(70,269)
Net Increase for period	(6,514)
Cash at beginning of period	23,362
Cash at end of period	16,848

Figure 4.1

Figure 4.2 shows the changes in the balance sheet between January and February that caused cash to go up or down.

Balance Sheet Comparison Approach

Balance Sheets	Month 1	Month 2	Cash Flow
ASSETS			
Current Assets			
Total Checking/Savings	23,362	16,848	
Total Accounts Receivable	697,598	753,414	(55,816)
Total · Inventory	639,144	651,257	(12,114)
Total Other Current Assets	675,641	687,679	
Total Other Current Assets	36,497	36,422	75
Total Current Assets	1,396,600	1,457,941	
Fixed Assets			
Total · Fixed Assets	13,208,857	13,208,857	0
Less Accumulated Depreciation	(7,373,675)	(7,398,463)	24,788
Total Fixed Assets	5,835,182	5,810,394	
Total Other Assets	72,287	73,483	(1,195)
TOTAL ASSETS	7,304,069	7,341,818	
LIABILITIES & EQUITY			
Liabilities			
Current Liabilities			
Total Accounts Payable	2,185,446	2,232,675	47,229
Total Credit Cards	174,387	173,030	(1,357)
Other Current Liabilities			
Total Other Current Liabilities	334,551	346,360	11,809
Total Current Liabilities	2,694,384	2,752,065	
Long Term Liabilities			
Loans Payable	1,810,682	1,763,220	(47,462)
Leases Payable	789,542	766,737	(22,806)
Total Long Term Liabilities	2,600,225	2,529,957	
Total Liabilities	5,294,609	5,282,022	
Equity			
3900 · *Retained Earnings	2,072,817	2,072,817	0
39000 · Common Stock	13,504	13,504	0
Net Income	(76,860)	(26,524)	50,336
Total Equity	2,009,461	2,059,797	
TOTAL LIABILITIES & EQUITY	7,304,069	7,341,819	

Cash Flow	(6,513)
Beginning Cash	23,362
Ending Cash	16,848
	16,848

Figure 4.2

Look at figure 4.2 to see how the significant drivers affected cash flow. The accounts receivable increased by $55,816 from month one to month two. When accounts receivable increase, your customers still have your money; therefore, an increase in accounts receivable decreases cash flow. This is why increases in assets are shown as negative changes (numbers in parenthesis). The person who collects your receivables is very important to your organization's cash flow. That person has to make sure your customers are not delinquent. It is very important for the company to be firm with your payment terms. If you decide your terms need to be thirty days, then enforce the thirty days religiously and have someone call your customers at the thirty-day point if you haven't been paid.

Inventory is the next area shown on the balance sheet. It increased by $12,113, representing a decrease in cash. This is why inventory control has its own chapter in this book. Too much inventory can devastate your cash flow. The following example illustrates two lessons.

REAL ENTREPRENEURIAL EXPERIENCE

Situation: A company had been awarded a potentially very lucrative Department of Defense (DOD) contract. Almost immediately after the contract award was announced, the COO ordered almost $1 million of steel directly from the mill. He got a 3 percent quantity price reduction and was delighted about the $30,000 that was going to drop directly to the bottom line through the cost savings of the purchase. It was not surprising to learn the COO received his bonus based solely on profits.

Issue: The DOD delayed the contract seven months leaving the company with a $1million bill with no revenue to produce the cash to pay for the steel. In addition, the DOD changed the specifications so some of the steel was unusable. Situation caused strained relationships with all vendors who couldn't get paid.

Resolution: Discipline established to not order before firm contract in hand, even if temporary layoffs were necessary while waiting for official go ahead.

Result: Created a cash flow oriented decision-making process. Improved relationships with vendors.

The most important aspect in business is cash flow. Do not jeopardize cash flow for the lure of increasing profit.

The next area is accounts payable, which increased by $47,229. An increase in accounts payable means you did not pay your vendors and kept the cash. A golden rule of business is *you cannot pay your vendors faster than you get paid.* Business is like a train, and you do not want to be the caboose. Several of your vendors probably don't pay much attention to their accounts receivable (what you owe them) until the invoices are more than sixty days old. You can perform a simple test to see how sensitive your vendors are to how timely you pay your bills. Cut the checks you normally do during a given week based on your vendors' normal terms, but don't mail them and see who calls.

Here are some of the comments from business owners as to why they don't want to slow payments to vendors:

1. We get product faster because we pay quickly.
2. My vendors are small companies and can't live with extended payments.
3. My vendors supported me during bad times.

These are wonderful thoughts, but they lie somewhere between not true and irrelevant. Vendors tend to respond to size. Vendors tend to respond to you based on how important a customer you are to them.

Dealing with small vendors can actually be dangerous to your business. If they stumble, you may fall. Finally, you must develop relationships with vendors so they know what is happening with your customers (payments to you are slowing down, business is starting to slow down or pick up, etc.). Your vendors must be able to support your timeline from sale, through production, delivery, and payment to you. If the vendors cannot support your timeline, you must either change your business model and/or get new vendors.

Fixed assets are the next area that can be a terrible drain on cash flow. The cash flow statements in figures 4.1 and 4.2 do not show any change in fixed assets currently. I selected the example below because of what this company had done in the past.

REAL ENTREPRENEURIAL EXPERIENCE

Situation: You can see from figure 4.2 that this company has over $13 million in fixed assets. You should also notice that the total liabilities are $5,282,022. The company borrowed tons of money to buy those fixed assets.

Issue: The total equity is $2,059,797. This means the liabilities are 2.5 times more than the total equity. Banks would not like this ratio. It is too high. This ratio and the fact that year-to-date net income is negative show that whatever the owner thought was going to be the result of buying all that equipment didn't work. Business owners can't build up capacity in anticipation of work that may not come.

Resolution: Renegotiated lease to improve cash flow. Sold some equipment, even if it was at a loss, to raise cash.

Result: Cash flow improved to the point it could keep the company alive.

Managing Cash Flow

So how do you control cash flow? First of all, you have to constantly track it. Here are two examples. The first example shows a day-to-day tracking of cash. The company has no line of credit and lives day to day based on what comes in and what clears the bank. The bank also participates in the flow of cash from time to time because some checks clear faster than anticipated and the bank advances the money to cover them for one day for a fee of $35 per check.

The second example seems more sophisticated because it involves a $9 million line of credit (LOC), but the company never has any cash because all money coming in goes into a lock box and reduces the LOC (See figure 4.6). The company has to draw money every week based on the covenants of the loan. (Kind of like asking for your allowance every week based on the number of chores you accomplished.)

Figure 4.3 shows the Excel form used to manage cash flow on a daily basis. You get started by listing all your vendors (yes, even if there are 225 vendors as in the company above, but you can probably download it from your accounting software). You also add loans, leases, rent, workout deals, payroll, and anything else that takes money from the company accounts. The trickiest part is you put entries into the spreadsheets when you think checks will clear (I told you this was the daily example.) You next color code when the checks actual clear (figure 4.3 uses shades of gray, but you should consider different colors) so you can go back and verify your assumptions about how long checks take to clear.

Daily Cash Flow	Day 1	Day 2	Day 3	Day 4	Day 5	Total
Vendor 1						
Vendor 2						
Vendor 10				$3,305		
Vendor 20	$479					
Vendor 33				$250		
Vendor 37				$7,307		
Vendor 102			$19,000			
Vendor 222					$116	
Total Vendors	$672	$366	$19,000	$10,962	$1,102	$32,102
Total Rent	$0	$0	$0	$0	$47,220	$47,220
Total Leases not EFTs	$0	$0	$0	$0	$0	$0
Loans:						
Loan 1						
Loan 2				$1,250		
Loan 3					$1,369	
Loan 4						
Loan 5	$500					
Total Loans	$500	$0	$0	$1,250	$1,369	$3,119
Total AP Debt	$0	$1,200	$4,464	$0	$0	$5,664
TOTAL VENDORS	$1,172	$1,566	$23,464	$12,212	$49,691	$88,105
PAYROLL	$7,000	$73,000	$0	$10,000	$6,000	$96,000
						$1,000
EFT						
Total Expenses	$8,172	$74,566	$23,464	$22,212	$56,691	$185,105
Customer 1	$16,737	$87,244	$0	$0	$24,643	$128,625
Customer 2	$0	$0	$0	$41,845	$0	$41,845
Custome 3	$4,765	$821	$0	$688	$0	$6,275
Customer 4	$3,384	$8,706	$0	$361	$0	$12,451
Customer 5	$148	$2,508	$1,112	$848	$2,998	$7,613
Other deposits						$0
Beginning Balance	($9,104)	$7,759	$32,472	$10,120	$31,650	$196,808
Projected ending bank balance	$7,759	$32,472	$10,120	$31,650	$2,599	
Checks outstanding	$0	$0	$0	$0		
	$7,759	$32,472	$10,120	$31,650	$2,599	

Figure 4.3

The following "Real Entrepreneurial Experience" uses the data from figure 4.3.

REAL ENTREPRENEURIAL EXPERIENCE

Situation: You can see in figure 4.3 that this company made it through the week with almost $2,600 in positive cash flow. A company bringing in almost $200,000 per week ($10 million annually) is squeaking out $2,600 in cash per week.

Issue: The company is walking a fine line and meticulous detail has to be paid to cash flow.

Resolution: The spreadsheet in figure 4.3 was created to make sure cash flow is managed.

Result: By managing cash flow on a daily basis, the company was given the time it needed to improve operations and explore other markets.

The next example I consider more sophisticated, but only because it involves the covenants of a bank line of credit. In the previous example, the cash flow was so weak that daily scrutiny was mandatory. The company using the system shown in figure 4.4 does not need daily scrutiny, but it has a complex situation with the bank that must be addressed. Figure 4.4 shows the first of three Excel spreadsheets necessary to use this different approach.

Cash Flow Projection for week of 1

	Projected WE 1		Actual WE 1		WE 2	WE 3
Beginning Bank Balance	(194,307)		(194,307)		-	-
Borrowing Base for Week	8,500,485		8,500,485		7,997,027	7,165,050
Previous Loan Balance	(8,374,081)		(8,374,081)		(8,053,312)	(7,723,552)
Projected AR Receipts	1,533,437		1,333,437		1,642,562	300,000
Projected other receipts	336,944		336,944		-	-
Projected Draws		1,381,825		1,349,612	1,312,801	824,174
Ending Loan Balance	(7,885,526)		(8,053,312)		(7,723,552)	(8,247,725)
Total Cash sources		1,187,518		1,155,305	1,312,801	824,174
Estimated Payroll for week		100,000		67,786	180,000	180,000
Minimum Bills		216,257		216,257	417,485	365,004
Vendor payments		871,261		871,261	715,316	279,170
Bank interest		-		-	-	-
Cash requirements for week		1,187,518		1,155,305	1,312,801	824,174
Ending cash balance		-		-	-	-
Loan Availability		5,242		(56,285)	(558,502)	(42,617)
Total Cash Availability		5,242		(56,285)	(558,502)	(42,617)

Figure 4.4

Look at the line labeled "Borrowing Base for Week." This refers to a Line of Credit (LOC), which allows borrowing against accounts receivable and inventory. It also has a lock box. A lock box means all the money from customers is sent directly to the bank (not the company) and immediately applied to reduce the LOC. The bank likes to sell this concept as minimizing the interest paid on the LOC. I prefer to describe a lock box as *you never have any cash.*

Figure 4.5 shows the programmed outflow of funds. Please note the area labeled "Vendor extensions past due date." Each vendor is analyzed with regard to how many days past their established payment terms they will unofficially allow your company to extend payments. These extensions are established by negotiations, trial and error, and begging and pleading. There is a basic theory at work regarding establishing these extensions. If you owe someone $10,000, they have some control of the rules over you. If you owe someone $500,000, you have some degree of control of the rules over them.

Vendors extensions past due date						3,782,251				871,261	715,316	279,170
	A	50										
	B	45										
	C	35										
	D	0										
	E	20										

Type	LOC	Date	Num	Name	Due Date	Terms	Open Balance	A-E	Ext	Revised Due Date	WE1	WE2	WE3
				Vendor 1			2,609				2,609		
				Vendor 2			1,200					1,200	
Bill	R	8/12	5318021	Vendor 3	10/11	Net 60	767	E	20	10/31	767		
Bill	R	9/11	5339595	Vendor 3	11/10	Net 60	2,466	E	20	11/30			
Bill	R	9/18	5339557	Vendor 3	11/17	Net 60	1,441	E	20	12/7			
Bill	R	9/18	5349825	Vendor 3	11/17	Net 60	750	E	20	12/7			
Bill	R	9/24	5340849	Vendor 3	11/23	Net 60	2,769	E	20	12/13			
Bill	R	9/30	5344462	Vendor 3	11/29	Net 60	4,899	E	20	12/19			
Bill	R	10/6	5350522	Vendor 3	12/5	Net 60	1,186	E	20	12/25			
Bill	R	10/6	5349578	Vendor 3	12/5	Net 60	3,431	E	20	12/25			
Bill	R	10/13	5352185	Vendor 3	12/12	Net 60	4,817	E	20	1/1			
Item Receipt	R	10/30	R912159	Vendor 3	12/29		3,165	E	20	1/18			
				Vendor 3			25,690				767	-	-
				Vendor 45			459,521				97,320	35,350	3,962
				Vendor 100			733,420				104,436	270,860	40,179
				Vendor 107			107,885				26,842	15,565	1,324
				Grand Total			3,782,251				871,261	715,316	279,170

Figure 4.5

All vendors (only slightly over 100 in this example) are listed and assigned a code A-E to extend the pay dates. You will also note the amounts owed to Vendor 45 and Vendor 100 are $459,521 and $733,420, respectively. These amounts are certainly significant (and dangerous), but it gets more interesting.

In figure 4.6, we take a look at the potential money coming in. Every potential source of funds is tracked. In addition, close attention must be paid to the rules of the line of credit.

	1-30	Contract 1 only 31-45	Contract 1 only 46-60	31-60	61-90	>90	TOTAL	% of Total AR	% over 90	Ineligible due to contract	Ineligible due to Aging
Contract 1											
8/29 Project 1		1,000,000			800,000		1,800,000				
10/17 Project 2	823,373						823,373				
Project 3			23,772		388,878	34,335	446,985				
8/14 Project 4		14,377	74,292		312,052	263,222	663,943				
Project 5	264,833	695,828	689,474		493,173	294,210	2,437,518				
10/17 Project4	146,424						146,424				
Project 6		552	216,126		4,614		221,292				
9/11 Project 7			0		97,656		97,656				
11/14 Expected pmt					(608,234)	(591,766)	(1,200,000)			5,876,270	
Total Contract 1	1,234,630	1,710,757	1,003,664	0	1,488,139	0	5,437,191	65%	0%	0	0
Contract 2											
10/24 Project 1	163,547					0	163,547				
Total Contract 2	163,547	0	0	0	0	0	163,547				0
Contract 3											
11/7 Project 1							0				
Total Contract 3	0	0	0	0	0	0	0				
Contract 9											
10/24 Project 1	129,672						129,672				
10/31 Project 2							0				
Project 3	0					0	0				
Project 4					971	2,350	3,321				
Total Contract 9	129,672	0	0	0	971	2,350	132,993				2,350
TOTAL	2,340,616	1,710,767	1,003,664	300,591	1,831,672	1,207,470	8,394,671			0.00	134,359

Notes

1. Any invoices that put one vendor's total greater than 70 percent of the total accounts receivable (ARs) are ineligible for borrowing base calculations.
2. All invoices that are more than ninety days old are ineligible for borrowing base calculations.

Less ineligible-concentration	0
Less cross aging	0
Less ineligible-aging	1,207,470
Add back XXX over 90	(1,073,111)
Total ineligible	134,359
Eligible AR	8,260,312
	0.8
AR Borrowing Base	6,608,250
	(250,000)
Sep Inventory including C&E %	1,638,778
Total borrowing base	7,997,027

Figure 4.6

Whether you have a line of credit or are just dealing with the cash payments, you must pay attention to when the money is coming in and going out.

Red Alert: Management of cash flow takes practice, discipline, and dedication. It is the most important business aspect for you to master

Mobley Matrix

I'm adding one thing that really isn't used in day-to-day business. It can be helpful for someone trying to understand the relationship between balance sheets, profit and loss statements, and cash flow. It is called the Mobley Matrix, developed by IBM's Lou Mobley. Figure 4.7 shows a Mobley Matrix. You actually read the matrix both vertically and horizontally.

The balance sheets, profit and loss, and cash flow statements are read vertically as you normally do. If you read horizontally, you can see how things interact. Look at the accounts receivable line. The starting balance is from last month's balance to which you add the sales and then subtract the collections. In this example, the collections were less than the sales; therefore, the accounts receivables went up.

	Beginning Balance Sheets	Income Statement	Cash Flow Statement	Ending Balance Sheet
ASSETS				
Current Assets				
Total Checking/Savings	23,362		Cash Increase (Decrease) (6,514)	16,848
Total Accounts Receivable	697,598	Total Income 791,491	Collections 735,675	753,414
Inventory	639,144	Material 183,220	Inventory Purchases 195,333	651,257
Current Assets	36,422			36,422
Total Current Assets	1,396,525			1,457,941
Fixed Assets	8,208,857		Fixed Assets Purchases 0	8,208,857
Less Accumulated Depreciation	(7,373,675)	Depreciation 24,788		(7,398,463)
Total Fixed Assets	835,182			810,394
Total Other Assets	72,287		Other Assets Purchases 1,198	73,485
TOTAL ASSETS	2,303,994			2,341,820
LIABILITIES & EQUITY				
Liabilities				
Current Liabilities		Direct Labor 161,073		
Accounts Payable	2,193,651	Other Direct Costs 75,171		2,232,675
Credit Cards Payable	174,387	Marketing & Sales 158,796		173,030
Other Current Liabilities	184,971	Administrative Expenses 138,103		186,578
Total Current Liabilities	2,553,009	Total Expenses 533,143	Expenses Paid 493,869	2,592,283
Loans Payable	1,536,045			1,515,134
Leases Payable	789,542		Repayments 43,716	766,737
Total Long Term Liabilities	2,325,587			2,281,871
Total Liabilities	4,878,597			4,874,154
Equity		Net Ordinary Income 50,340		
Retained Earnings	(4,638,966)			(4,638,966)
Common Stock	13,504		Distributions 8,967	13,504
Paid in Capital	2,127,720		Other payments 5	2,119,653
Net Income	(76,860)	Net Other Income (5)		(26,525)
		Net Income 50,335		
Total Equity	(2,574,603)		Free Cash Flow (6,513)	(2,532,334)
TOTAL LIABILITIES & EQUITY	2,303,994			2,341,820

Figure 4.7

To summarize, underscore, and highlight, cash flow is indeed the most important thing for a business owner to master. It doesn't matter what size your business is, you must look at cash flow at least weekly.

Unfortunately, in situations where the company is under financial duress cash flow must be looked at daily. The fact of the matter is the larger your business gets, the more serious the problems that can develop if you do not watch cash flow. It's not fun, but it is critically important.

CHAPTER 4 HIGHLIGHTS

1. Cash flow is indeed the most important aspect for a business owner to master.
2. Decide how frequently you need to review cash flow (start with at least weekly) and stick to that timetable religiously.

CHAPTER 5

INVENTORY

As discussed in chapter 4, inventory is one of the four major drivers of cash flow. Inventory control is also critical to operational efficiency. This is why inventory has its own chapter because of the three major areas we are examining —*cash flow, operational efficiency, and business model* —inventory affects two of them.

We will divide inventory into two categories —raw material inventory needed to build something and finished goods inventory available for sale. Inventory is a two-headed monster. How well you buy it affects your profit and loss statement. How much you buy affects your cash flow. Many entrepreneurs do not pay nearly enough attention to this critical area of inventory.

Let's start with raw material inventory. The hardest scenario is when a business builds a lot of different models or versions or sizes of its product that requires different materials. When I ask business owners why they build so many types or versions, they usually answer that they can't say no to their customers. What they don't do is analyze what should be a special order that supports a higher price. But let's get back to the bread-and-butter inventory material. Avoid the mistake of tying up too much cash in sitting inventory by turning over raw material inventory as quickly as possible.

Inventory Turnover

You can calculate your inventory turnover as follows:

Inventory turnover = $\dfrac{\text{Material costs of goods sold}}{\text{Average Inventory}}$

Here are some real numbers. If your material costs of goods sold for a year was $3 million and your average inventory level was $600,000, then:

$$\text{Inventory turnover} = \frac{\$3,000,000}{\$600,000} = 5$$

To look at it another way, the number of days it takes to sell your inventory is:

$$\text{Inventory days} = \frac{365}{\text{Inventory turnover}} = \frac{365}{5} = 73$$

This means it takes almost 2.5 months to sell your inventory. Is this bad or good? It depends on several things, but certainly two very important issues are how long it takes to get your inventory and how long it takes to make your product. What would be the effect of raising your inventory turnover to 7.5? To raise your inventory turnover to 7.5 with the same sales, your equation would have to look as follows:

$$\text{Inventory turnover} = \frac{\$3,000,000}{\$400,000} = 7.5$$

This would mean you would have get your inventory more quickly and have it more "just in time". Is it worth trying to do? Changing your average inventory by $200,000 means you have $200,000 more in cash available to do whatever you wanted to do with it — new marketing campaign, more R&D, or even to take out of the company. It sure is worth investigating.

Whoever is in charge of ordering your material should be able to do the following:

1. Look constantly for sources of the quality product you want at the best price and terms.
2. Negotiate with vendors to have what you need whenever you need it.
3. Have a way to determine how much you use of what, so you know what you need.

In addition to using computers to control inventory, you also must physically control it. There should be a particular place to store each piece of inventory and that inventory should be in its place. Hunting for inventory because it is in whatever space was available is a tremendous waste of labor hours.

REAL ENTREPRENEURIAL EXPERIENCE

Situation: A company put six different categories of toys they could use in their product mix. The goal was to mix the quantities of each component to produce an average cost of $1.65 per component. The table in figure 5.1 below illustrates the mixture:

Cost	Quantity	Total
$1.15	5	$5.75
$1.30	4	$5.20
$1.60	7	$11.20
$1.90	3	$5.70
$2.60	1	$2.60
$3.75	1	$3.75
	21	$34.20
Average Cost	=	$1.63

Figure 5.1

Issue: The inventory turnover was 3.5, indicating way too much cash in inventory and no one knew why.
Resolution: The answer was they were *not* purchasing based on the usage by class. In other words, they would order the same number of $1.15 items as $1.60 items as $3.75 items. They actually used seven times as many of

the $1.60 items as they used of the $3.75 items when they made their product. The ordering procedures were changed.

Result: Inventory reduced by $400,000. Inventory-handling labor greatly reduced.

Let's talk about the inventory of finished goods for resale. Suppose you don't make things, but buy things manufactured by others, then sell them to others. How many of those products do you keep in inventory? First of all, you need to know what gross profit you make on each product.

Many entrepreneurs do not track how they make their gross margin; they keep track of how much they sell of each product. *Unfortunately, it is not sales that make net profit, its gross profit that makes net profit!*

Prove it to yourself. Buy something and then sell it for 25 percent less than your cost. Advertise like crazy, and your sales will go through the roof and you will lose money on every sale. Making money is about *gross profit*, not sales.

Rank everything you sell by the total gross profit each item produced during the last twelve months. Find the break points at which you generate 80 percent and 90 percent of the gross profit. Eliminate those products in the last 10 percent and see how much money you can free up.

REAL ENTREPRENEURIAL EXPERIENCE

Situation: An individual store owner who sold products for a national supplier was short on capital and long on inventory. The owner had an exclusive territory, like a franchise owner.

Issue: In most cases, it would be to the store owner's advantage to open a second store on the other side of the territory but there was no capital to do so.

Resolution: Store owner ranked all products in inventory by the total amount of gross profit that product produced during the last twelve months. The table in figure 5.2 shows a summary of those results:

# of Products	Gross Profit	%	Value of Inventory
1,900	$3,085,233	80.00%	$1,871,564
1,436	$385,606	10.00%	$182,541
11,514	$385,606	10.00%	$832,035
14,850	$3,856,445	100.00%	$2,886,140

Figure 5.2

There are a total of 14,850 different products with a value of $2.8 million. That fact in itself is staggering. The gross profit produced by those products for the last twelve months was $3.85 million. The next staggering fact, but not an unusual one was that *80 percent of that gross profit was produced by only 13 percent (1900) of the products.* In addition, 11,514 products contributed only 10 percent of the gross profit.

Result: The national company repurchased most of the slow moving inventory. The individual store owner freed up over $500,000 in cash and opened a new store. Today, the owner has more market share out of his territory and makes significantly more net profit because the owner paid attention to inventory.

As stated in Chapter 4 – Cash Flow, inventory is one of the major drivers for maximizing cash flow. Proper inventory control will also increase operational efficiency. It is well worth managing aggressively.

Red Alert: Inventory control is very mathematical and should be done without much emotional involvement. It also can require some tough discussions with vendors. When you learn how to ask vendors for the moon, the worst you'll probably get will be much better than what you have. Aggressive inventory management will free up a lot of cash.

CHAPTER 5 HIGHLIGHTS

1. Understand the importance of just-in-time inventory and make it happen.
2. Have a specific place to store your inventory and store it in that place.
3. Calculate the gross profit of every item you sell. It will allow you to make better inventory decisions.

CHAPTER 6

YOUR FINANCIAL INFORMATION AND YOUR COMPANY'S PERFORMANCE

If you really want to make your dream come true you must know what your financial information tells you about the performance of the company and how to fix when if it needs fixing. Not being able to do this is a fairly consistent weakness of entrepreneurs. Most entrepreneurs think one of the following, which are faulty at best and untrue at worst:

1. The business will be successful because of the technical details of their amazing product.
2. The sales-oriented entrepreneurs are thinking about how they can sell anything to anyone no matter what the economy is doing.
3. The entrepreneurs who are currently making a lot of money without knowing much about financial information think things won't change.

Here is the real truth:

1. Entrepreneurs who build a business and sell it to achieve their own financial independence are hard working, did whatever they did at the right time, and had luck on their side. The vast majority of entrepreneurs are not sophisticated CEOs who would be hired by Fortune 500 companies to run their companies.

2. Most entrepreneurs are not financial experts.
3. Most entrepreneurs do not know what they do not know.
4. 90 percent-plus of all business are exactly the same. They sell something to generate revenue, they have costs of material and people to produce that revenue, they realize a gross profit to cover the administrative expenses of running a business, and they need to make a decent profit as reward for taking the risk of running a business. They also have to keep monitoring costs of goods sold and administrative costs and continually reduce those costs.

Your financial statements and your key performance indicators are the things that tell you where operational efficiencies can be improved. These statements and indicators will also tell you if the changes you made are working.

Although I always thought financials were important, the concept that financial expertise was the key to success was driven home when I was introduced to an organization called Contractor Success Group (CSG). This was a heating and air conditioning (HVAC) industry association that taught residential sales and service companies how to make more money. What I discovered after meeting some of the members was that many of the most successful owners of these businesses were former accountants, not HVAC experts. They simply followed the time proven approach that had worked before. They were very diligent in achieving the necessary financial and operational metrics taught by CSG. What they were doing is not too different from successful franchisors. If you follow the franchisor's operations manuals, you will be successful.

I want my message to be *very clear*. If you get the proper financial information and know what it is telling you, the following will come true:

1. You will be able to tell what areas of your business need improvement.
2. You will be able to reduce costs, including taxes.
3. Your business will be more competitive.
4. Your business will more easily weather economic downturns.
5. The value of your business will increase.
6. The chances of achieving your dream dramatically improve.

Importance of Understanding Direct Costs

The way to apply this philosophy to your business is to start with the basics of the profit and loss (P&L) statements. Here are the basic parts of the P&L:

> +Revenue
> <u>-Costs of Goods Sold</u>
> Gross Profit
> <u>-Administrative Expenses</u>
> Net Profit

Your key to success is *gross profit, not revenue*. You want to keep gross profit high and administrative expenses low. It seems simple. The first step is to make sure you put all the direct costs of selling your product or service into costs of goods sold (COGS).

Here's a listing some of those direct costs:
1. Material purchased to make your product
2. Factory labor to make your product
3. Factory management to produce the product
4. Employment benefits for factory employees
5. Lease payments on factory equipment
6. Depreciation on factory equipment
7. Equipment rental used in production
8. Freight in and out
9. Repair and maintenance labor
10. Repair and maintenance of equipment
11. Workers compensation insurance for factory and maintenance people
12. Shop supplies
13. Pro rata portion of rent for factory
14. Pro rata portion of utilities for factory
15. Sales salaries, wages, and commissions
16. Direct marketing used to get customers
17. Installation wages and cost of installation of your products
18. Delivery expenses

In other words, any costs you would not have if you weren't selling a product or service. This is where service organizations get into trouble. Because they provide services through people, they record very little in the way of COGS and put all the people-related costs below the gross profit line. It makes it very hard for them to discover if they are really making any money providing a particular service.

This format does not meet all the rules of GAAP (Generally Accepted Accounting Principles). You know what? *I don't care*. Your accountant doesn't have the responsibility to run your company. These are internal documents. If you have audited or reviewed statements, your accountant can change the statements to any format they want. The format that is recommended in this book will better help you to achieve your dream.

When you are disciplined about placing all the direct costs into COGS, then everything else becomes administrative expenses (or indirect expenses, if you prefer). The largest Administrative expenses tend to be the rest of the rent and the people who support those folks who make the product or provide the service. You must constantly work to keep these expenses minimized.

Before we go on, we must take a side trip to talk about variable costs and fixed costs. Not all COGS are variable (remember we put part of the rent up there, which doesn't change based on sales). On the other hand, not all administrative expenses are fixed. That being said, to demonstrate why you must concentrate on gross margin, we are going to assume all COGS vary with sales and all administrative expenses are fixed. You need to know the revenue point where all COGS and administrative expenses are covered.

Understanding the Breakeven Point

Shown below is the breakeven point for revenue of $266,667, which produces a net profit of $0:

Revenue	$266,667	100%
COGS	$186,667	70%
Gross Profit	$80,000	30%
Admin Exp	$80,000	30%
Net Profit	$0	0%

Figure 6.1

Above this point in revenues, things get interesting. Please note the gross profit percentage is 30 percent.

Look what happens as sales increase above breakeven:

Revenue	$266,667	100%	$340,000	100%	$380,000	100%	$420,000	100%	$430,000	100%
COGS	$186,667	70%	$238,000	70%	$266,000	70%	$294,000	70%	$301,000	70%
Gross Profit	$80,000	30%	$102,000	30%	$114,000	30%	$126,000	30%	$129,000	30%
Admin Exp	$80,000	30%	$80,000	24%	$80,000	21%	$80,000	19%	$80,000	19%
Net Profit	$0	0%	$22,000	6%	$34,000	9%	$46,000	11%	$49,000	11%
Increase in revenue			$73,333		$40,000		$40,000		$10,000	
Increase in net profit			$22,000		$12,000		$12,000		$3,000	
% of every sales dollar dropping to the bottom line			30%		30%		30%		30%	

Figure 6.2

For every dollar increase in revenue, the net profit increases by 30 percent. So for every dollar increase in revenue above breakeven, the gross profit produced by those dollars drops to the bottom line. Read that last sentence again. Life is good.

I used an example that simplified things by dividing the variable and fixed arbitrarily. For your actual business, you must code every line item as fixed or variable and then calculate your company's breakeven point.

The next lesson in reading P&L statements is to look at both absolute dollars and percentages together. Figure 6.3 shows a company's P&Ls side by side (some months and account codes purposely hidden to make a difficult spreadsheet somewhat easier to read.) You should receive your monthly financial statement along with this side-by-side representation *each and every month.*

Detailed Analysis of a Profit & Loss Statement

Profit & Loss Statement	Jan	100%	Feb	100%	Apr	100%	Jun	100%	Aug	100%	Sep	100%	Nov	100%	Dec	100%	Full 12 months	100%	Average
Total Income	860,126	100%	752,813	100%	955,408	100%	997,811	100%	900,978	100%	923,985	100%	743,055	100%	743,101	100%	10,520,321	100%	876,693
Cost of Goods Sold																			
49999 - Beginning Inventory	577,899	67.2%	483,285	64.2%	728,787	76.3%	716,808	71.8%	602,251	66.8%	643,463	69.6%	579,444	78.0%	695,935	93.7%	577,899	5.5%	
51990 - Ending Inventory	(483,285)	-56.2%	(736,043)	-97.8%	(750,940)	-78.6%	(663,811)	-66.5%	(643,462)	-71.4%	(658,537)	-71.3%	(695,935)	-93.7%	(619,887)	-83.4%	(619,887)	-5.9%	
50000 - Purchases	214,710	25.0%	224,386	25.0%	284,376	29.8%	257,009	25.8%	265,112	29.4%	282,512	30.6%	254,632	34.3%	218,174	29.4%	2,953,836	28.1%	246,153
50500 - Labor	187,688	21.8%	162,493	21.6%	279,620	29.3%	150,288	15.1%	155,781	17.3%	252,518	27.3%	161,008	21.7%	216,702	29.2%	2,156,901	20.5%	179,742
51500 - Other Costs	66,047	7.7%	68,366	9.1%	102,342	10.7%	103,158	10.3%	82,188	9.1%	93,530	10.1%	64,700	8.7%	65,363	8.8%	878,912	8.4%	73,243
52000 - Measure	13,191	1.5%	22,411	3.0%	29,297	3.1%	18,884	1.9%	20,198	2.2%	29,733	3.2%	25,252	3.4%	28,973	3.9%	268,324	2.6%	22,360
52100 - Installers	55,711	6.5%	40,778	5.4%	78,440	8.2%	63,177	6.3%	56,781	6.3%	81,990	8.9%	48,529	6.5%	66,724	9.0%	696,327	6.6%	58,027
52200 - Delivery	13,429	1.6%	14,370	1.9%	22,153	2.3%	17,910	1.8%	17,208	1.9%	28,100	3.0%	16,811	2.3%	22,415	3.0%	221,580	2.1%	18,465
52400 - Other Costs, Measure & Install	13,401	1.6%	9,510	1.3%	17,509	1.8%	12,004	1.2%	15,325	1.7%	23,433	2.5%	14,253	1.9%	19,348	2.6%	177,915	1.7%	14,826
55009 - Sales Expenses	87,199	10.1%	105,291	14.0%	138,302	14.5%	90,548	9.1%	104,078	11.6%	91,095	9.9%	60,827	8.2%	74,546	10.0%	1,049,450	10.0%	87,454
55999 - Marketing Expenses	1,069	0.1%	313	0.0%	0	0.0%	5,707	0.6%	2,622	0.3%	4,615	0.5%	2,144	0.3%	3,036	0.4%	27,282	0.3%	2,274
Total COGS	747,059	86.9%	395,159	52.5%	929,886	97.3%	771,682	77.3%	678,081	75.3%	872,452	94.4%	531,665	71.6%	791,329	106.5%	8,388,539	79.7%	699,045
Gross Profit	113,066	13.1%	357,654	47.5%	25,522	2.7%	226,129	22.7%	222,897	24.7%	51,534	5.6%	211,389	28.4%	(48,228)	-6.5%	2,131,782	20.3%	177,649
59999 - Administrative Expenses																			
60000 - Advertising	0	0.0%	25	0.0%	100	0.0%	100	0.0%	100	0.0%	25	0.0%	50	0.0%	25	0.0%	600	0.0%	50
60010 - Auto Expenses	5,926	0.7%	2,433	0.3%	2,334	0.2%	1,216	0.1%	816	0.1%	171	0.0%	464	0.1%	90	0.0%	16,925	0.2%	1,410
60030 - Bank Charges	9,284	1.1%	6,320	0.8%	6,159	0.6%	4,038	0.4%	3,717	0.4%	3,305	0.4%	1,982	0.3%	1,463	0.2%	51,894	0.5%	4,324
60200 - Insurance Expenses	4,738	0.6%	3,318	0.4%	28,762	3.0%	26,059	2.6%	5,164	0.6%	11,374	1.2%	10,888	1.5%	15,413	2.1%	155,718	1.5%	12,976
60210 - Interest Expense	18,833	2.2%	17,350	2.3%	19,193	2.0%	22,209	2.2%	10,629	1.2%	10,552	1.1%	9,832	1.3%	26,742	3.6%	197,893	1.9%	16,491
60220 - Leases, Office Equipment	2,888	0.3%	2,354	0.3%	3,061	0.3%	2,180	0.2%	2,256	0.3%	2,174	0.2%	2,160	0.3%	2,042	0.3%	29,648	0.3%	2,471
60230 - Legal, Accounting, Professional	3,879	0.5%	6,470	0.9%	17,137	1.8%	19,771	2.0%	54,207	6.0%	35,855	3.9%	17,276	2.3%	(13,291)	-1.8%	225,329	2.1%	18,777
60240 - Licenses & Permits	983	0.1%	150	0.0%	1,171	0.1%	6,903	0.7%	1,814	0.2%	1,845	0.2%			566	0.1%	15,691	0.1%	1,308
60340 - Rent Expenses	44,949	5.2%	44,949	6.0%	44,949	4.7%	(611)	-0.1%	44,949	5.0%	44,949	4.9%	38,207	5.1%	39,217	5.3%	457,792	4.4%	38,149
60350 - Repairs & Maintenance	1,043	0.1%	1,043	0.1%	1,043	0.1%	1,043	0.1%	1,043	0.1%	1,043	0.1%	1,043	0.1%	1,043	0.1%	12,517	0.1%	1,043
60370 - Taxes Expenses	4,749	0.6%	4,835	0.6%	5,378	0.6%	45,061	4.5%	3,671	0.4%	12,426	1.3%	4,131	0.6%	26,817	3.6%	110,980	1.1%	9,248
60390 - Telephone Expenses	865	0.1%	9,602	1.3%	5,185	0.5%	5,209	0.5%	5,338	0.6%	5,301	0.6%	4,103	0.6%	4,299	0.6%	61,055	0.6%	5,088
60410 - Utilities	8,934	1.0%	7,759	1.0%	8,955	0.9%	9,036	0.9%	8,937	1.0%	10,014	1.1%	8,246	1.1%	8,804	1.2%	106,534	1.0%	8,878
60420 - Wages	32,406	3.8%	31,026	4.1%	42,523	4.5%	27,346	2.7%	30,998	3.4%	52,123	5.6%	38,274	5.2%	51,987	7.0%	427,948	4.1%	35,662
Total Administrative Expenses	159,055	18.5%	152,913	20.3%	203,274	21.3%	188,050	18.8%	189,974	21.1%	210,980	22.8%	153,894	20.7%	182,374	24.5%	2,076,073	19.7%	173,006
Net Ordinary Income	(45,989)	-5.3%	204,741	27.2%	-177,752	-18.6%	38,079	3.8%	32,923	3.7%	-159,446	-17.3%	57,495	7.7%	(230,602)	-31.0%	55,709	0.5%	4,642
Net Other Income	(5)	0.0%	(5)	0.0%	(5)	0.0%	(5)	0.0%	(5)	0.0%	(5)	0.0%	(5)	0.0%	8,232	1.1%	15,639	0.1%	1,253
Net Income	(45,994)	-5.3%	204,736	27.2%	(177,757)	-18.6%	38,074	3.8%	32,918	3.7%	(159,451)	-17.3%	57,490	7.7%	(222,371)	-29.9%	70,753	0.7%	5,896

Detailed Analysis of a Profit & Loss Statement

Figure 6.3

The main reason for this format is it invites the following questions: Do you really believe such and such is true? If so, why?

We are going to look at individual items that should drive you to ask these questions. I will not tell you what the answers are in most cases because I want you to concentrate on why you should ask the question.

You will find that in business it is more important to know what questions to ask and when to ask them than to think you need to know all the answers yourself.

Asking the Correct Questions

Take this quiz.

Do you believe that ....

1. ... the bank charges of $9,284 in January are reasonable?
2. ... the telephone bill was only $865 in January?
3. ... the net income was really $204,736 in February in a month where the total income was the third lowest of the year at $752,813?
4. ... there was an inventory increase over $250,000 (from $483,285 to $738,043) in February?
5. ... it cost $18,000 more in sales expenses to sell $100,000 less in February than January?
6. ... telephone expenses went from $865 in January to $9,602 in February?
7. ... it was reasonable for direct labor to increase from $162,493 in February to $279,620 in April?
8. ... insurance expenses jumped from $3,318 in February to $28,762 in April?
9. ... administrative wages went from $31,000 in February to over $42,000 in April?
10. ... June was the highest total income month at $997,811, yet only produced net income of $38,074?
11. ... rent was a credit of $611 in June?
12. ... taxes were $45,061 in June, more than nine times any previous month?

13. ... insurance expenses dropped from $26,059 in June to $5,164 in August?

14. ... $54,207 in legal, accounting, and professional in August was justified?

15. ... insurance expenses dropped from $28,059 in June to $5,164 in August?

16. ... installers were paid $66,724 in December when only $48,529 was spent in November for the same income?

17. ... interest expense jumped from $9,832 in November to $26,742 in December?

18. ... this is a profitable business with $70,753 in net income for the year when there was a contribution of $250,000 to the profit in February from an inventory increase?

It is only by asking these kinds of questions that you truly discover how your business is running and what you need to change. Did the bookkeeper make some technical errors? Not as many as you think. The truth is you *must be able to look through the numbers* to see what is going on. Unless you practice doing this or are working with someone who is very good at it, you may get in financial trouble before you fully realize what is going on.

> **Red Alert: Review your financial statement by generating questions as shown above. Do at least three reviews with an expert or until you come up with the same questions the expert does.**

CHAPTER 6 HIGHLIGHTS

1. Make sure you are getting accurate financial information.
2. Put all direct costs above the gross profit line.
3. Understand what your breakeven point is and keep working to reduce it.
4. Learn how to ask the correct questions about your financial statements.

CHAPTER 7

YOUR BUSINESS MODEL

Business owners must constantly challenge their business model. Simply stated, nothing lasts forever. A major issue occurs when the current model had some degree of success and the owners are reluctant to change. Because business owners are working hard on the current model, they are not spending enough developing a new model.

Let's start with a list of well known companies that did not change their business model: Pan American World Airways, Wang Laboratories, Lionel Corporation, F.W. Woolworth Company, Bethlehem Steel, Converse, Montgomery Ward, Polaroid Corporation, Adelphia, WorldCom, Tower Records, NetBank, The Sharper Image, Silicon Graphics, Blockbuster, and Borders Group.

You probably have heard of most of these companies. I didn't have to go back past 2000 to extract this small list of the companies that declared bankruptcy. Some of these companies were giants but are virtually nonexistent today.

What all business owners must ask themselves are the following questions:

1. Is my business somehow more protected than these businesses were?
2. Are there forces at work beyond my control that are hurting my current business model?
3. As a business owner, am I smarter than all the people running the above companies?

IBM

It's very possible the greatest model change in history has been at IBM. IBM has been around a long time. It invented the hard disk drive in 1956, which still exists in computers today. IBM is responsible for barcodes, magnetic strips on credit cards, and even time clocks. It was a machine-producing machine.

In the early 1990s, nothing was going right for IBM. It was losing tons of money and running out of cash. Louis Gerstner became CEO on April Fools' Day 1993, (see circle on chart) which should have given him a chuckle. The chart below shows the IBM stock price increase reflecting his amazing success, but what did he do?

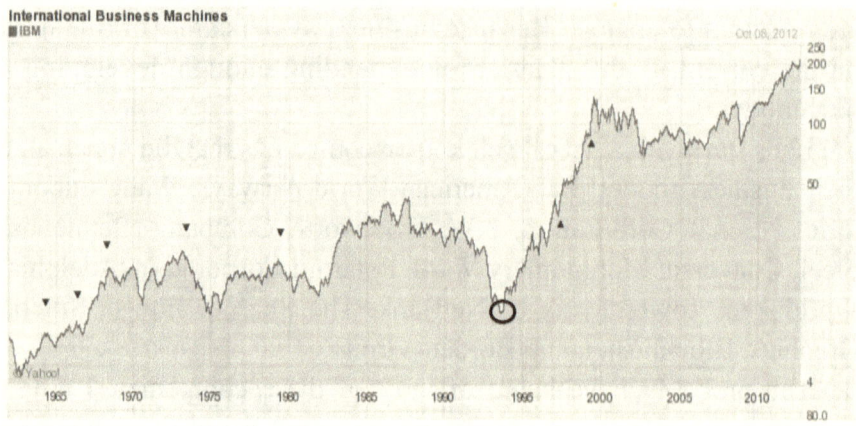

Figure 7.1

Gerstner changed most things. As an outsider, he had no emotional attachment to long suffering products. This is a valuable lesson for you, as a business owner, to learn. Make sure you are getting input from outsiders who are not emotionally attached to your products and services, but who want you to succeed.

IBM doesn't focus on products and devices any longer. Today, 84 percent of IBM's profits come from software and services. Its pre-tax profit margin has risen from 13.9 percent in 2000 to 20.2 percent today. It is a completely different company from what it was in 1993.

Applying the IBM Lessons to Your Company

Since this book is aimed at owners of businesses with revenue from $5 million to $50 million, some owners in this group may think it is hard to take lessons from a giant such as IBM, but it really isn't. What IBM did can be summarized as follows:

1. Got outside help from someone who had no emotional investment in what IBM was currently doing.
2. Made the business solvent by cutting costs and by selling assets to raise cash.
3. Jettisoned lower margin, timing consuming products for higher margin software and services.
4. Changed the compensation structure to reward internal cooperation and performance.
5. Changed company focus to be customer driven, instead of being preoccupied with the company.

When put in these terms, all the above items can be applied to any size business.

Changing the business model starts with an analysis of which products and services provide the highest gross margin. Chapter 5 emphasizes this analysis to optimize inventory. This analysis is also critical for examining how effective the current business model is working.

Too often owners state they have to sell the low margin products or services to provide full service to their customers. It is not surprising when these owners discover the majority of their business becomes selling low margin products or services.

Some businesses actually increase overhead expenses to enable them to sell lower margin products or services. This move simply makes changing the business model harder, not easier.

Chapter 6 discusses the importance of understanding accurate, reliable financial statements. The numbers in accurate, reliable financial statements don't lie. They tell the owners what products and services are truly making money.

One example of a company in this book's target revenue range, started out by supplying a web-based, organizational assessment tool.

After a successful fight to avoid bankruptcy, the owners discovered the highest gross profit came from consulting assignments, not when customers used or purchased the tools. They deemphasized the tool sales, but raised the price to make whatever sales took place worth the trouble. They then concentrated on consulting. The company was stabilized and changing their business model gave them far more options to future growth.

Owners make changing their business models more difficult when they leverage the business too much. Many times this happens due to real estate and equipment purchases. The business can't handle any downturn during the transition because the business must pay for the owner's purchases. The owners try to keep the old model working at the current level while trying to change to the new approach. This duality almost never works. Owners must be prepared for sales and profit to go down before the new approach takes hold.

Let's look at another example. A company did an excellent job refurbishing metal lab furniture. They expanded into medical lab planning and custom fume hoods. They were very lucky because they discovered the lab and fume hood work was extremely profitable at the same time the Chinese started making metal furniture more cheaply than this company could refurbish old furniture. Even though they were lucky these things happened simultaneously, they still fought the idea of abandoning what got them started (refurbishing metal lab furniture). Most owners find the existing business deteriorating before they start to look for the better path, if they ever do.

When starting to examine the current business model, as owner, you should start the deliberations with a question. If you had to start from scratch, what business would you be in? If it is at least remotely close to what you do now, you are in luck. If it isn't, you're not going to like the message, which is to sell the current business (or pieces of it) and get started on the new business.

Next, the owner must start to outline what are the different products and services that are going to be offered. List the expected gross profit percentage of each of these products and services. Then, the owner must determine if the business has the correct staff to provide the new products or services.

Did any of the people who owned the businesses on the bankruptcy list make money? One that jumps to mind is Wayne Huizenga at Blockbuster. After building Blockbuster to billions in revenue, he sold his interest. Huizenga is rich, Blockbuster is virtually nonexistent.

Chapter 9 — The End Game discusses selling the business to achieve your dream. Business is a means to an end. The end is your dream. There are two lessons from Blockbuster that every business owner needs to learn:

1. The vast majority of businesses will not last forever. There is a lot of risk in sustaining a business.
2. When the value of your business achieves the value needed to achieve your dream, sell it.

Please don't plan (or expect) that your business model will remain successful until you decide you want to stop. Changing your model will most likely not only be necessary, but also a continuous process.

CHAPTER 7 HIGHLIGHTS

1. Business owners must recognize it is highly improbable that their original business model will last until they achieve their dream.
2. To maximize the changes of achieving their dream, business owners must constantly update their business models.
3. Use the lessons from the IBM example to change your business model.

CHAPTER 8

PRICE INCREASES AND DISCOUNTS

A critical part of changing your business model is a total understanding of pricing and whether or not to use discounting. It is fascinating to see businesses quick to give discounts and scared to death about price increases without paying any attention to the mathematics involved with each. Of course to do the math correctly, you must know the individual cost of goods sold (and, therefore, the gross profit) for each product under consideration. Knowing what the gross profit of each product or service is a recurring theme in this book.

Price Increases

Look at the following example:

Before price increase	
# of units sold	1,000
Price per unit	$100
Sales	$100,000
Cost of goods sold per unit	$70
Gross profit per unit	$30
Gross profit in dollars	$30,000

Figure 8.1

You need to determine the percentage reduction in sales you can afford to absorb and still make the same number of gross profit dollars. To do that, expand the table to:

	Before price increase	After price increase
# of units sold	1,000	750
Price per unit	$100	$110
Sales	$100,000	$82,500
Cost of goods sold per unit	$70	$70
Gross profit per unit	$30	$40
Gross profit in dollars	$30,000	$30,000

Figure 8.2

What does this table tell you? If you raised the price of the product 10 percent (from $100 to $110) and only sell 750 instead of 1,000, *you make the same number of gross profit dollars.* A reduction in sales of 250 units (1000-750) would mean you would have to lose 25 percent of your sales. Unless you are trying to compete as the low cost provider, you probably won't lose that much business. If you are trying to compete as the low cost provider, change your business model because you will eventually be crushed. You don't have to start with a 10 percent price increase, but try something to test what I am saying.

The key, of course, is that your cost of goods sold per unit remains exactly the same when you raise the price. Now you may say cost of goods sold will increase with the price increase because your sales people work on commission. You just solved another issue. You should not pay salespeople based on gross sales. You should pay them based on gross *profit*.

Price Increase Calculations

I know you don't want to hit and miss on the where the breakeven point is, so I am giving you this formula:

$$Y = \frac{P}{P + (1 - C)}$$

Where P equals the percentage price increase, C equals the cost of goods sold percentage, and Y equals the percentage decrease in sales that you can take, and you still make the same gross profit dollars.

So let's look at plugging in the numbers of the previous example with a price increase of 10 percent and the cost of goods sold percentage of 70 percent. The formula looks as follows:

$$Y = \frac{.1}{.1 + (1 - .7)} = \frac{.1}{.1 + (.3)} = \frac{.1}{.4} = .25 = 25\%$$

You must do this calculation for each individual product because I guarantee you all your products do not have the same gross profit.

There is another positive side effect of raising prices. That is you will probably eliminate bad customers. First, we have to define bad customer.

There is general agreement that bad customers have the following characteristics:

1. They purchase your lowest margin products.
2. They pay slowly.
3. They treat your employees poorly.
4. They take up a lot of your employees' time.

Which customers are most likely to stop purchasing from you if you raise your prices? Your bad customers. So let's look at the probable outcome of the price increase:

1. You make at least the same number of gross profit dollars with fewer sales.
2. You have bad customers go away.

Not a bad outcome for something you have to do anyway. What I mean by "have to do anyway" is that you always have to strategically be raising prices. The main reason is your costs are going up. Oil price increases affect not only your transportation costs, but also your cost of plastics and grains.

Throw health care costs and workers' compensation insurance costs in the mix, and I probably don't need more to convince you that your costs are constantly going up.

I can't leave the price increase section without addressing how often you should raise prices. Here's a look at how *not* do to it. You probably received a letter from a supplier that starts off something like this: "Because you are a good customer, we have tried to hold off passing on our cost increases to you, but we now have to raise our prices 6 percent." How did you feel about that notification? Most people don't like it.

Raise prices slowly and more often. Customers usually don't freak out at 1.5 – 2 percent price increase done every six months. Let's examine a case where the owner talked himself into delaying a price increase even though his customers were actually expecting one.

REAL ENTREPRENEURIAL EXPERIENCE

Situation: The price of oil was reaching $150 per barrel. This business delivered its product daily to his customers throughout southern California. The cost of gasoline had been steadily increasing over twelve months.

Issue: Transportation costs were rolled into the price of this company's product. The owner was scared that if he raised prices, his customers would buy from the competition. The company kept taking loses because of something over which they had no control — gasoline prices.

Resolution: A letter was set to existing customers announcing a price increase due to the increase in gas prices.

Result: One customer called and stated he couldn't believe the increase didn't take place a year ago. The appropriate gross profit was restored across the product line.

> **Red Alert: Increasing prices is scary, but it must be done. You must know the gross margin that each product or service produces. If done correctly, the increase will move dollars directly to your bottom line. Done incorrectly, the increase may cause you even greater problems.**

Discounts

Unless you are trying to dump inventory that will become obsolete, discounting is usually not a good idea. Has your sales team ever come to you and stated that if you lowered the price they could sell a lot more of a particular product? Do the math to see what you are facing. Start with the same situation used in figure 8.1:

Before discount	
# of units sold	1,000
Price per unit	$100
Sales	$100,000
Cost of goods sold per unit	$70
Gross profit per unit	$30
Gross profit in dollars	$30,000

Figure 8.3

Then see what needs to happen with a 10 percent price discount to maintain the same gross profit dollars:

	Before discount	After discount
# of units sold	1,000	1,500
Price per unit	$100	$90
Sales	$100,000	$135,000
Cost of goods sold per unit	$70	$70
Gross profit per unit	$30	$20
Gross profit in dollars	$30,000	$30,000

Figure 8.4

Yes, you are reading the chart correctly if you noticed a *50 percent increase in sales* is necessary to maintain the same gross profit dollars! How many of your salespeople will agree to a 50 percent increase in the number of units they will be able to sell? Probably none.

Discount Calculations

The formula to calculate the percentage increase in sales necessary to just maintain the same gross profit dollars is:

$$Y = \frac{P}{(1-C) - P}$$

Let's again plug the numbers for this example of a 10 percent discount with the same cost of goods sold percentage of 70 percent:

$$Y = \frac{.1}{(.1 - .7) - .1} = \frac{.1}{(.3) - .1} = \frac{.1}{.2} = .5 = 50\%$$

I have to address the issue of thinking that you made discounting decisions because things were bad, and you had to cover overhead. Unfortunately this thinking probably signifies the start of a downward cycle from which your current business will not recover.

Red Alert: If you are discounting, you probably have a lot of work to do regarding changing your business model. Discounting will lead you down a road to a place you really don't want to be. Continuous discounting will lead to a continuing decline in the value of your business.

CHAPTER 8 HIGHLIGHTS

1. Calculate the consequences of raising prices.
2. Raise prices in smaller increments, but do it more frequently.
3. Don't discount unless you are trying to get rid of inventory you probably won't use.

CHAPTER 9

THE END GAME

Why do you own a business? Here are a few reasons owners give:
1. I had a great idea.
2. I want to be my own boss.
3. I'm good at what I do.
4. I can't stand working for someone else.

For most entrepreneurs who know what they are doing, their business will be the main source of capital to achieve their financial independence dream. In many cases, the business represents the preponderance of their net worth. So what is the end game? The end game is to build the business to the value needed so selling it yields the capital needed to accomplish the owner's dream.

Your Capital Needs

The first step is to figure out how much capital you need to provide a standard of living you want *for the rest of your life*. One way is to create an Excel spreadsheet like the one in figure 9.1. What questions do you need to answer? Only the following four:

1. How much inflation adjusted, after-tax income do you need for the rest of your life to maintain the standard of living you desire?
2. How many years do you want that income to last?
3. What is the inflation rate you want to assume?
4. What is the after-tax rate of return on your investments you want to assume?

When you start to think about these questions, you will realize they are *not easy*. Figure 9.1 was developed using the following answers:

1. $200,000
2. 40 years
3. 3 percent
4. 4 percent

With these answers, let's see how much capital you need. Figure 9.1 shows the detailed calculations to determine the amount of capital needed to produce an inflation adjusted income level of $200,000. What does that really mean? First of all, note that the income level goes up by 3 percent every year.

Next, note at the fortieth year the amount you consume is $633,405, which will be the inflation adjusted equivalent of $200,000 forty years in the future. The first head shaking reaction is, "I won't ever need that much." Do the math. Look historically at what things cost. It's for your own protection. If you don't want the inflation protection, then pick zero for the inflation rate.

The next thing to notice is that you are completely out of money after forty years. This is not some scheme to make your heirs rich. I agree that your spending may go down, but you can always reduce the target amount if you wish. It is basically a mathematical calculation based on your assumptions. Here are some cautions:

1. Don't make the time period too short (don't run out of money before you run out of life).
2. Don't make the after-tax investment rate of return too high (how did your investments do during the decade of 2001 through 2010?).
3. Don't make the inflation rate too low (especially the way we are going when this book was written).

Doing the Calculations

Inflation adjusted, after tax income		$200,000
Number of years		40
Inflation Rate		3.00%
After-Tax Rate of Return on Investments		4.00%
Capital needed		$6,667,508

Year	Capital at beginning of Year	Used	Capital at end of Year
1	$6,667,508	$200,000	$6,467,508
2	$6,726,208	$206,000	$6,520,208
3	$6,781,017	$212,180	$6,568,837
4	$6,831,590	$218,545	$6,613,045
5	$6,877,567	$225,102	$6,652,465
6	$6,918,563	$231,855	$6,686,709
7	$6,954,177	$238,810	$6,715,366
8	$6,983,981	$245,975	$6,738,006
9	$7,007,527	$253,354	$6,754,173
10	$7,024,339	$260,955	$6,763,385
11	$7,033,920	$268,783	$6,765,137
12	$7,035,742	$276,847	$6,758,896
13	$7,029,251	$285,152	$6,744,099
14	$7,013,863	$293,707	$6,720,156
15	$6,988,963	$302,518	$6,686,445
16	$6,953,903	$311,593	$6,642,309
17	$6,908,001	$320,941	$6,587,060
18	$6,850,543	$330,570	$6,519,973
19	$6,780,772	$340,487	$6,440,285
20	$6,697,897	$350,701	$6,347,196
21	$6,601,083	$361,222	$6,239,861
22	$6,489,456	$372,059	$6,117,397
23	$6,362,093	$383,221	$5,978,872
24	$6,218,027	$394,717	$5,823,309
25	$6,056,242	$406,559	$5,649,683
26	$5,875,670	$418,756	$5,456,915
27	$5,675,191	$431,318	$5,243,873
28	$5,453,628	$444,258	$5,009,370
29	$5,209,745	$457,586	$4,752,159
30	$4,942,246	$471,313	$4,470,933
31	$4,649,770	$485,452	$4,164,318
32	$4,330,890	$500,016	$3,830,874
33	$3,984,109	$515,017	$3,469,093
34	$3,607,856	$530,467	$3,077,389
35	$3,200,485	$546,381	$2,654,104
36	$2,760,268	$562,772	$2,197,495
37	$2,285,395	$579,656	$1,705,740
38	$1,773,969	$597,045	$1,176,924
39	$1,224,001	$614,957	$609,044
40	$633,406	$633,405	$0

Figure 9.1

So what does this have to do with your business? Most likely you will have to sell your business for enough to net the needed capital to produce the income you need. But there is one more calculation you need to do. Remember the sale of your business will be subject to income taxes. So for how much do you have to sell your business to produce the needed capital after the income taxes are paid? At the time this chapter was written, the capital gains tax rates were 15 percent. If you are lucky enough that those rates are still in place and you live in a state which also has income taxes, you best use at least a 20 percent income tax rate (at a minimum) on the sale of your business. Therefore, using the example in figure 9.1 where you need $6,667,508 to produce your income goals, you best use $8,334,385 as the target sale price of your business (if you sell your business for this amount and are taxed at 20 percent, you will net the needed capital).

Calculating the Value of Your Business for Planning Purposes

To get a ballpark estimate of what your business is worth, you must calculate your company's EBITDA (Earnings before Interest, Taxes, Depreciation, and Amortization). EBITDA is calculated as shown below:

> Earnings (net income)
> + Interest deductions paid
> + Income taxes paid
> + Depreciation deductions
> + Amortization deductions
> EBITDA

Assuming you are using a five times EBITDA multiple for the value of your business (Caution — research is recommended before you make this assumption), your business will need to produce an EBITDA of $1,666,877 to get a sale price of the needed $8,334,385 to net what you need. (When you do this, please use round numbers, like $8.5 million and $1.7 million, for your goals).

This means you have to manage your business to produce the needed EBITDA. You have to have a business plan that increases sales with the right kind of product mix to produce the gross profit to yield the right EBITDA to get where *you* said you wanted to go.

There is one more piece of information you need to understand, but you will not like to hear. *Most business owners do not sell their businesses when they are worth the most.* Why is this statement a fact? Because running a business when it is at the top is easy. Owners start to think they are really good at running a business.

Here are two examples to drive this point home. The first is the residential construction industry during the period 2004 through 2008. Anyone even remotely associated with this industry during 2004 through 2006 made a tremendous amount of money. Most thought they were really good. They were hiring people, expanding into areas in which they had no expertise, and buying more real estate to support their growth. Then it happened — the real estate market collapsed. Owners realized they could not make a profit at lower revenue levels. Competition got more ruthless, so owners lowered their prices, which caused them to lose money on many of the jobs they bid. They could not support all the overhead, including the extra real estate they purchased. They finally realized they were more lucky than good during the boom times. They faced the reality that *business has risks the owner cannot control.*

The next example will look at how many businesses crashed and burned after they were on top. We can go back as far as the best buggy whip company that didn't believe the automobile was here to stay. Speaking about autos, how about the Big Three auto makers? They couldn't be beat by those crummy foreign cars, right? How about the airlines? Orville and Wilbur are probably turning over in their graves. What about those mortgage companies that couldn't loan money fast enough? How many banks are not around anymore? IBM doesn't make computers anymore (they were smart enough to completely change their business model). Are you smarter than all these folks?

For your own protection, you should sell your business when it reaches the value that will produce your financial independence. Business is risky —quit as soon as you can achieve your dream and consider yourself very lucky.

CHAPTER 9 HIGHLIGHTS

1. Establish how much your business needs to be worth to achieve your dream.
2. Make sure you are working on your business to make it worth what you need it to be.
3. When you get the business to where it needs to be, *Sell it —Do Not Hesitate.*

CHAPTER 10

BANKS

If you want to achieve your dream, you absolutely need a good banking relationship.

Banks are in business to make money, just as you should be. I have met a lot of very nice business bankers. Unfortunately, banking is a lot harder since the great bailout of 2008. The government rules that banks now have to follow mean that money is actually tighter and harder to get. This means that business owners have to put their businesses in a position where many banks want their business.

Look for a bank when your financials are strong, not when you are weak. There is another very important thing you must remember: Most bankers have never run a business. If you get outside the norms or ratios, the bank has established (or been forced to), their hands will be tied and so will yours.

There are a lot of things to consider when interviewing a bank. That is correct. If you put your business in the correct position, you are interviewing them, not the other way around. Remember to ask for everything at the beginning, whether you currently need the services or not. The beginning of the relationship is probably your strongest negotiating position. Don't waste it. Here are some of the things to consider in your interview:

1. **Lines of credit** — Probably one of the key ingredients in a business banking relationship, especially if you want your business to grow. Make sure you understand what determines the interest rate on the line of credit. (For instance, I never met

a business owner who told me he was glad he did an interest rate swap.) It seems that fixed interest rate loans are a thing of the past. With a variable loan, look at the long-term volatility of the benchmark.

How is the borrowing base determined? Here are the major items that determine how much you will be able to borrow:

a. Percentage of accounts receivable – Try for 85 to 90 percent. Be very careful of the restrictions, such as receivables that are ninety days past due don't count; if more than a certain percentage of one customer's accounts receivables are past ninety days, none of that customer's accounts receivables count toward the borrowing base. The receivables from one account can't represent more than 70 percent of all receivables (this can be a real problem when you have a major account that is a slow pay).

b. Percentage of inventory – Try for 60 percent. Banks don't like to deal with inventory because it is sometimes hard to liquidate near full value quickly. The one very real exception is wood. Raw lumber can be liquidated near 100 percent of its value, so use that in the negotiations if you have a lot of lumber.

c. Work in Progress (WIP) – Try for 35 percent. Banks don't like WIP because they can't finish it themselves and then sell it. This will be a tough one.

d. Finished goods – Try for 60 percent as long as all you have to do is ship it or install it. Try to get the value that's based on the price to your customer, not the cost carried on balance sheet.

Try to negotiate that the cash paid to you does not automatically reduce the loan balance. The bank will argue that it reduces the interest you pay. What it means is that you never have cash and can't get any if you are temporarily out of borrowing base compliance.

2. **Term loans** — Part of your overall borrowing facility with a bank should be a term loan. This will actually be harder than you think, but it is absolutely worth fighting for. Try for a five-year term loan at a fixed interest rate. Try for a term component even if you have to reduce the variable interest rate line of credit amount (which most likely the bank will demand).

3. **Personal Guaranties** — The bank will ask you sign a personal guarantee where all your personal assets are available to them. This is because the bank wants a second source of repayment. Try to limit the amount of your personal assets. For instance, if you have significant personal assets, try to exclude your residence as collateral. Since you will most likely have to sign the guarantee, get in writing what you need to do to get released from the guarantee. You won't like the answer because it will be something like the business will have a tangible net worth greater than what they are loaning you. In other words, when you don't need the loan anymore, they will release you from the personal guarantee.

4. **Loan Renewals** — Every time the bank renews the loan, they charge you a fee. Why? You didn't negotiate something different at the start. Does it really cost them what they charge you? See if you can negotiate the renewal time period to be at least two years and try to pre-negotiate a nominal fee.

5. **Don't necessarily put all your business with one bank** — This is definitely counterintuitive. Normally you get your best deal by giving someone more business. You have to look at protecting yourself and your business. For instance, most business owners are convinced that it is better to own than rent, because everyone knows you build equity if you own and real estate always goes up (or does it?). If you have both your line of credit and your real estate loan with the same bank, it is very hard to get concessions on the real estate loan without the bank somehow affecting your line of credit. It can get worse as described in the following "Real Entrepreneurial Experience":

REAL ENTREPRENEURIAL EXPERIENCE

Situation: A company had a $9 million line of credit with a regional bank. The owner decided to buy a second manufacturing facility. He formed a partnership with a friend to own the building and got an $11 million loan for the real estate from the same regional bank.

Issue. The owner thought the bank would look at the real estate as being the source of security for that loan and the business as being the security for the business line of credit. The bank made the business guarantee the real estate loan. The loan was made to the partnership in which the business had no ownership.

Resolution. Absolutely none.

Result. The owner is locked into his current bank until the real estate recovers. When that occurs the owner should try to refinance the real estate loan elsewhere so the business can deal cleanly with the original bank based on the business needs.

You can do your own math to see if your business is bankable. See figure 10.1 to see the minimums you'll need.

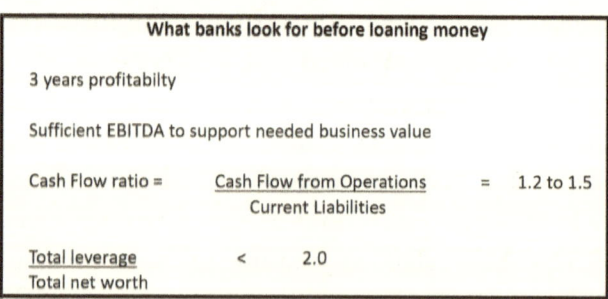

Figure 10.1

Red Alert: Don't kid yourself about being bank-able if you don't meet these conditions. Having to resort to a factoring company *is not* being bank-able. Fix the business so you can shop banks.

REAL ENTREPRENEURIAL EXPERIENCE

Situation: The owners of a business that was still in its infancy decided they were worth more than the company could afford to pay them.

Issue: They accrued what they wanted to be paid, thereby driving the profitability very negative, and put the unpaid wages as a debt on the balance sheet. When they went to a bank, they were turned down, of course, because they never showed a profit.

Resolution: Restructured the balance sheet and converted the liabilities to owners to equity.

Result: Offered a relationship from three banks.

At the time of the writing of this chapter, banks were under more scrutiny than ever. It doesn't make them better bankers. It doesn't make things better for business. It makes things much harder. Money is tighter at the very time business needs more options. Government (and greed) got us here and you, as the business owners, are expected to get us out of this mess. Business owners must be better than ever to get what they want from banks.

CHAPTER 10 HIGHLIGHTS

1. Understand the environment in which the banks are forced to operate.
2. Fix your business so you can have banks competing for your business.

CHAPTER 11

RETIREMENT PLANS

Why is it necessary to discuss retirement plans in a book about how business owners can achieve their dreams through their businesses? The reason is businesses owners spend too much time and money on retirement plans that provide little or no help in them achieving their dreams. In addition, some business owners do things that could actually put them in jail.

Defined Benefit Plans

Let's review where business has been with retirement plans. I'll start with the Defined Benefit Plan. This is the biggie where all the employees received a specific percentage of their salary *for the rest of their lives*, starting at the specified retirement age. There were all sorts of rules I won't go into, but it was indeed a golden handcuff to keep employees. Why would one leave and give up the retirement plan?

Some of the more famous defined benefit plans are the U.S. military (twenty years of service and you get 50 percent of your salary), U.S. Postal Service, many U.S. cities and states, and, of course, General Motors. With the possible exception of the U.S. military (but now the powers in Washington are trying to change it), all public and private companies are running as fast as they can to close down all of these plans to new employees or have the employees pay a higher percentage of their wages to fund the plans. Why?

The amount of money the employer is required to contribute is a function of the assumed and actual rate of return the plan assets earn. The decade from 2001 through 2010 was very unkind to these plans because they actually lost money. The employers were then required to contribute considerably more money into the plans to make up for the shortfalls of the investments. An article in the March 5, 2012, *Bloomberg Business Week* stated that General Electric, Boeing, and 3M must make contributions of $400 billion from 2011 through 2015 to ease underfunding. Now that is not what shareholders want to hear. In addition, the retirees are living longer than the actuarial tables said they would. Oops. There goes another good idea. So good-bye to the biggest golden handcuff—the defined benefit pension plan.

REAL ENTREPRENEURIAL EXPERIENCE

Situation: The owner of the company (I'll call it Company A) was paid through a separate corporation (Company B) owned by someone Company A's attorney could control. The owner of Company A actually was not an employee of his own company, but performed management services through the Company B for Company A. Company B established a defined benefit retirement plan. The owner of Company A was the only participant in the Company B's plan. Company A had no plan for its employees.

Issue: The whole arrangement violated the intent of the law. There were never any underfunding problems because in a one-person plan, you can change the assumptions every year to match whatever the company is able to do. Company B kept changing the contribution calculations to fit whatever the owner of Company A needed even though he didn't own a single share of stock of Company B.

Resolution: Absolutely none. The owner and attorney believe they have enough smoke and mirrors that they won't get caught.

Result: Status quo for now

Profit Sharing Plans

We also had era of profit sharing plans. The theory was that if the employees did a great job, and the company produced profits, then there would be money to put into the profit sharing plan for the employees' benefit. There would be no contribution needed by the employees. The percentage of profits along with the investment performance theoretically should be enough to provide the employees with a nice nest egg. What could go wrong with that approach? First, did the employees truly understand how what they did really contributed to the profits? In addition, if an employee did a great job, did he get more of a reward than someone who didn't do a great job? The answer is no to both questions. The contribution made to the profit sharing plan on the employees' behalf was a percentage of salary. The government rules regarding how much could be put into the plan on behalf of the employees actually worked against both the lowest paid and the highest paid. The profit sharing plans started out with a maximum contribution of 15 percent of wages. Now 15 percent of wages scared a lot of employers, so they wanted the option for a lower number and the plans were written so the contribution was not mandatory; it was voluntary at the employer's discretion.

An employee who made $30,000 per year got a contribution of $4,500 per year. If that employee worked for the company for twenty years and the investments in the plan averaged a compounded 7 percent annual return, the employee would have less than $200,000. I don't want to sneeze at $200,000, but one should ask, "Who works for a company for twenty years today and can retire for the rest of their lives with only $200,000?" But the biggest issue in the decade beginning in 2000 arose when profits weren't enough to continue to fund the plans and the investment results were terrible. So good-bye profit sharing plans.

REAL ENTREPRENEURIAL EXPERIENCE

Situation: When this company was doing well, it made large contributions to a profit sharing plan. A series of poor business decisions was followed by a downturn in the economy. The company lost a significant amount of money for several years in a row.

Issue: As business continued to decline, the owners borrowed money from the profit sharing plan. The owners were also participants in the profit sharing plan, so they took money out of their accounts. They took far more money out of the plan than was allowed as loans. But they didn't stop there. They took an equal amount from the employees' accounts. In addition, the 5500 (profit sharing plan tax return) was filed three months late without a mandatory audit.

Resolution: A leading ERISA attorney was hired to negotiate with the Department of Labor (DOL) regarding the $45,000 fine the DOL had assessed. To replace the employees' money, the wife of one of the owners was terminated so she could get access to her 401k plan funds. She gave her distribution to her husband who put the money back into the profit sharing plan. (The wife still works at the company for no pay. Talk about taking a hit for the team.) The audit was performed and the 5500 was refiled.

Result: The attorney negotiated the penalty down to $15,000 to be paid over three months. The DOL is happy; the administrator is happy; and the owners are happy they didn't face any charges. You can't make this stuff up.

401k Plans

Then came the onslaught of 401k plans. The 401k plan was probably the greatest marketing job that was ever done by mutual funds. The better 401k plans were structured based on variation of the following premise:

1. The employee contributes up to 6 percent of salary on a pretax basis.
2. The employer matches 100 percent of the employee's contribution up to 3 percent of employee's compensation.
3. The employee chooses the investment from the family of mutual funds.

What could go wrong with this approach? For one thing, when did employees learn the best way to invest money? All you have to do is steadily invest through payroll deductions and dollar cost averaging evens out the hills and valleys of the markets. Right? Wrong. The first thing that went wrong is that many companies experienced problems so they had to stop matching the employees' contribution. That meant the employees were on their own with their pretax contributions *and then the markets crashed.*

REAL ENTREPRENEURIAL EXPERIENCE

Situation: A nice little business was growing and decided to set up a 401k plan to reward the employees. The business owners started to ignore increasing costs. Bills were past due.

Issue: The owners withheld the employees' 401k plan contributions from their paychecks, but didn't put the money into the 401k plan. They used the money to pay bills instead.

Resolution: The owners were forced to cut their own salaries by 50 percent. The money was used to repay the 401k plan until it was paid in full. Everything was working until one day when the receptionist yelled out, "Who wants to take a call from the California Employment Development Department (EDD)?" The EDD was told that the situation would be corrected by September 1.

Result: The EDD called on September 2. All the money had been placed into the 401k plan. The owners were very lucky that a plan with a definitive deadline had been established.

Red Alert: You don't need a retirement plan to keep employees. It's nice, but not mandatory. Pay top wages; expect top performance; share the winnings. Don't screw with the IRS or the Department of Labor. The risk is not worth the reward.

Employee Stock Ownership Plans

So where is this whole retirement plan thing going? It is my personal belief that if the United States is going to get back to being competitive, employees will need ownership. If the employees are partial owners, there is a better chance they will make decisions that make the business more successful. Is this some socialistic idealism in line with President Obama's thinking? Quite the contrary; it is a sophisticated, business technique with income tax incentives for a business owner to use to reduce his own risk and allow for diversification of his assets.

The leveraged Employee Stock Ownership Plan (ESOP) is an underutilized tool for businesses. An ESOP is a tax qualified, defined contribution, employee benefit plan that invests primarily in the stock of the sponsoring company.

Paige Ryan of ESOP Services, Inc. provided me with the genesis of figure 11.1.

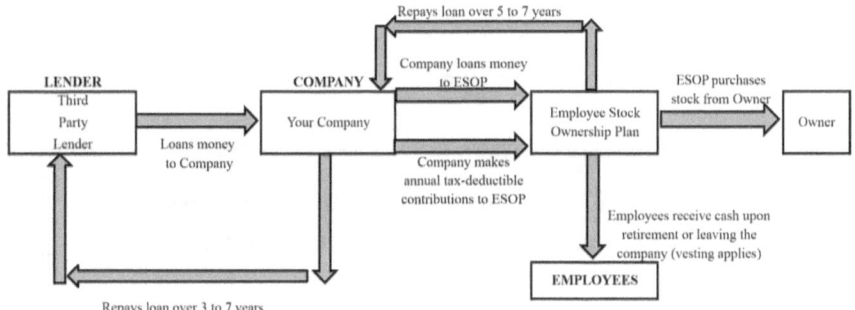

Figure 11.1

The simple summation for this transaction is the owners of the business sell at least 30 percent of their stock to the employees using borrowed money. The company actually borrows the money and most likely the owners have to guarantee the loan. The company makes fully tax deductible contributions to the ESOP annually, which at least covers the annual amount of the loan repayment (seven-year terms are doable). The beauty of this arrangement is all the interest *and principle amounts are tax deductible.* When was the last time you got a loan where the principle payments were tax deductible?

The owners now have taken some risk money off the table because they have sold 30 percent of their business. The 30 percent has been sold to the employees who now have a very big motivation to improve the business. It gets even better. The owners (if a C corp) can elect to defer gain on the sale of their stock sold to an ESOP by reinvesting all of the proceeds in Qualified Replacement Property (QRP). QRP is stock or debt instruments of a domestic operating corporation. If you don't like those types of investments, most brokerage firms will let you borrow money and use the QRP as collateral.

Let's look at an example. You own a company that is worth $10 million. Your company borrows $3 million and loans it to the ESOP, which buys 30 percent of your stock. The owner buys QRP with the

$3 million. The company needs to make contributions to the ESOP of approximately $440,000, which cannot exceed 25 percent of payroll, requiring an annual payroll of $1.76 million. The company now has a new deduction of $440,000 to reduce income tax exposure. The ESOP makes a loan payment to the company, which is passed on to the original lender.

The owner now has 30 percent of his money that can be diversified *away from the risk of the business*. The employees now own part of the company and can see a reason to start thinking more like owners.

Red Alert: ESOPs are complicated and expensive, but the rewards can be fabulous. Get expert help.

CHAPTER 11 HIGHLIGHTS

1. Figure out a reward system that enables employees to think like owners.
2. Take some of your risk money off the table when you can. There is too much risk in running a business to think the glory days will last forever.

CHAPTER 12

GET HELP WITH YOUR FIX

People who aim at nothing usually hit it. Having a dream helps you focus on what needs to be done to achieve your dream. Owning your own business should help in achieving the owner's financial independence. If you master what I told you in this book, you will greatly increase the chances of your business being worth what is needed to achieve your dream.

The key will be to have access to people who have the actual experience of doing what I have outlined. Realize your business is not unique. Surround yourself with advisors who have more experience in business than you do. Ideally these people will have run several different types of businesses.

I finished writing this book after 2012 Olympics were completed. There was not one interview during the Olympics where I heard these world-class winners say, "I did it all by myself; that is why I won." With the right help, you can have a business that is the means to an end —achievement of your financial independence.

As was pointed out in the very beginning of the book, no one can go it alone. Every business owner should have a board of advisors. This is way beyond a recommendation. *It is a strong belief, supported by experience and data.*

Vistage International is a worldwide company comprised of more than 16,000 business leaders in fifteen countries. I had the privilege of being a member for fourteen years. Vistage did a study in 2010 that showed that during the five years from 2005 through 2009, businesses with an advisory group grew 15 percent more than the average Dun &

Bradstreet U.S. company. Given the terrible economic environment in 2008 and 2009, these are incredible results.

What kind of advice should you seek? You are looking for "this is how to run your business better and make it more valuable" advice. The right people to give you this type of advice are:

1. People who have run more businesses than you have.
2. People who have run larger businesses than you have, but not too big (Executives from billion-dollar companies don't know the challenges entrepreneurs face.)
3. People who will tell you the positives and negatives about your issue and then give their recommendation(s) with the reasons.
4. People who will tell you when you are doing the wrong thing and help you find the right thing. (This is tough love and you are probably not used to it.)

The Biz Fix was written to help you greatly increase the chances of business owners achieving their financial independence dreams. Chances are you don't know what needs to be fixed in your business. Get the right help and make your dream come true.

ABOUT THE AUTHOR

Nicholas R. Duva is the CEO of Bonduva, Inc., a turnaround and management consulting firm. He has been the interim CEO or COO of eleven different companies, of which four were sold. He also has provided financial and operations improvement consulting to hundreds of other companies.

Duva started his career in the U.S. Air Force launching Titan III missiles and procuring the F-15 aircraft. He then moved to the aerospace industry, remaining in aircraft development. These experiences gave him a solid foundation in the systems approach for problem solving.

Duva has lived in the owner's shoes every day dealing with all aspects and pressures of business. Having run everything from a start-up firm to a $150 million consolidation, he has dealt with problems in all business functional areas. Duva has masters' degrees in systems management and electrical engineering. He was a member of the international organization of business leaders, Vistage International, for fourteen years.

Services provided by Bonduva, Inc.

Management Consulting: Analyze the strength and weaknesses of businesses and help the owners with whatever degree of *The Biz Fix* is required.

Turnaround Management: For those businesses operating under duress, Duva negotiates with vendors, banks, and even employees to get the business stabilized. Establishes appropriate degree of cash flow management, improves operational efficiency, and examines and updates the business model.

Member of the board of advisors: Duva attends quarterly meetings with other trusted advisors to assist owner to:

1. Establish strategic objectives.
2. Develop processes to enhance ability to achieve objectives.
3. Create appropriate action items and timelines.
4. Help owner maintain ferocious discipline and focus.

Veteran CEO coach on your shoulder: A unique Bonduva service, which is more one-on-one with the owner, but requires some explanation. Suppose you were a basketball coach and could meet Mike Krzyzewski (2012 Olympics and Duke) once per month to talk about your team. Suppose you were a football coach and could call up Bill Belichick (New England Patriots) anytime you had an issue about football to discuss.

The relationship with Duva is not a "rah-rah" relationship. The purpose is to enable business owners to achieve their dreams by making their businesses more valuable. This package includes the following:

1. Monthly review of the financials
2. Unlimited telephone calls on any business challenge
3. Unlimited emails on any business challenge

4. At least one half-day meeting per month

5. Time table for all action items with two-way accountability

Bonduva, Inc. is dedicated to helping business owners achieve their financial independence dreams.

Contact Information

Nick Duva
nduva@san.rr.com
858-459-0158

www.ingramcontent.com/pod-product-compliance
Lightning Source LLC
Chambersburg PA
CBHW022022170526
45157CB00003B/1325